ART QUILT
PORTFOLIO

People & Portraits

ART QUILT
PORTFOLIO

People & Portraits

PROFILES OF MAJOR ARTISTS

•

GALLERIES OF INSPIRING WORKS

Martha Sielman

LARK
CRAFTS
Asheville

EDITOR: **Amanda Carestio**

PRODUCTION EDITOR: **Julie Hale**

ART DIRECTOR: **Shannon Yokeley**

ART PRODUCTION: **Kay Holmes Stafford**

COVER DESIGNER: **Shannon Yokeley**

ON PAGE 2:
Lora Rocke
One Last Look 1952, 2010

FRONT COVER:
Maria Elkins
Windblown, 2011

BACK COVER, CLOCKWISE FROM BOTTOM:
Lora Rocke
Bowling Team Toast, 2008

Jenny Bowker
Abu Ali and the Gilded Chairs, 2009

Colette Berends
Mother, 2008

Joan Sowada
Fresh Outlook, 2006

FRONT FLAP:
Yoshiko Kurihara
Morning Breeze, 2009

BACK FLAP:
Leni Wiener
Crosswalk, 2011

SPINE:
Alice M. Beasley
Entre Nous, 2010

LARK CRAFTS
An Imprint of Sterling Publishing
387 Park Avenue South
New York, NY 10016

© 2013 by Lark Crafts, an Imprint of Sterling Publishing Co., Inc.

ISBN 978-1-4547-0351-8

Library of Congress Cataloging-in-Publication Data

Sielman, Martha.
  Art quilt portfolio : people and portraits : profiles of major artists, galleries of
inspiring works / Martha Sielman. -- First Edition.
    pages cm
  Includes index.
  ISBN 978-1-4547-0351-8
  1. Art quilts--United States--Themes, motives. 2. Portraits on quilts. I. Title.
  NK9112.S494 2013
  746.460973--dc23
      2012028088

Distributed in Canada by Sterling Publishing
c/o Canadian Manda Group, 165 Dufferin Street
Toronto, Ontario, Canada M6K 3H6
Distributed in the United Kingdom by GMC Distribution Services
Castle Place, 166 High Street, Lewes, East Sussex, England BN7 1XU
Distributed in Australia by Capricorn Link (Australia) Pty. Ltd.
P.O. Box 704, Windsor, NSW 2756, Australia

For information about custom editions, special sales, and premium
and corporate purchases, please contact Sterling Special Sales at
800-805-5489 or specialsales@sterlingpublishing.com.

Email academic@larkbooks.com for
information about desk and examination copies.
The complete policy can be found at larkcrafts.com.

Manufactured in China

2 4 6 8 10 9 7 5 3 1

larkcrafts.com

CONTENTS

INTRODUCTION

I GREW UP IN HUNTINGTON, ON LONG ISLAND, and one of my favorite pastimes was to go with friends by train into New York City in order to window-shop. The train trip took an hour and gave me the perfect opportunity for people-watching as passengers got on and off at the many stops along the way. I liked to imagine what their stories were, what had formed the lines on their faces and shaped their appearances. I often wished I had a secret camera so that I could capture an expression or a face that seemed particularly filled with personality.

This book has allowed me to fulfill some of that old desire. Though other artists have captured their likenesses, I enjoy looking at the people depicted on these pages and imagining their histories.

We're hardwired from birth to recognize human faces, and we continue to concentrate on them throughout our lives. A face is a point of connection, an indicator of emotion and intent. Sometimes we over-generalize and see a face where there's no actual person present, a phenomenon known as pareidolia—the tendency to interpret vague images as specific ones. Car designers often rely on this phenomenon: the shape and placement of taillights and fenders can create subtle expressions that may appeal to consumers. The best-known example of pareidolia is probably the Man in the Moon.

This focus on facial recognition is what allows us to look at the portraits in this collection that are composed of unusual colors (a face that's half purple and half yellow) or patterns (faces made with polka dots or zebra stripes) and not only see faces but realize that they convey certain emotions or resemble people we know. Many of the artists in this book make use of our ability to see faces despite their lack of realism and enjoy choosing fabrics that are full of surprises.

The *Art Quilt Portfolio* series debuted in 2012 with *The Natural World*. *People and Portraits* is the second entry in the series. In a book of this type, the images need to be grouped so that the reader has a framework for viewing them. When I began considering images for this collection, I thought that perhaps I could organize them by age or gender, but it quickly became apparent that those categories missed something essential to the spirit of the art. I ended up with categories that celebrated the emotional truth of the portraits: happiness, contemplation, community, icons (figures from history and literature), family and friends, work and play. The gallery sections of this book display the work of 120 artists, while a more in-depth treatment is given to the quilts created by 21 featured artists, showing several pieces by each coupled with interviews describing their backgrounds and working methods.

The 21 featured artists live in Australia, Canada, Denmark, Italy, Japan, the Netherlands, Sweden, and the United States. They approach the task of capturing the human spirit from a wide variety of viewpoints, using a range of techniques and materials. Some of the artists, such as Cheryl Dineen Ferrin and Leni Wiener, document the people that they see around them: Cheryl records her fellow motorcycle riders, and Leni captures the people she encounters on the streets of New York. Artists like Lora Rocke and Colette Berends focus on the past. Lora bases her work on her collection of old photos, while Colette recalls the glamour and elegance of her life as a nightclub entertainer.

TERRIE HANCOCK MANGAT ● ESME, 2011 ● 57 x 50 inches (144.8 x 127 cm) ● Cotton, silk, acrylic paint, cotton thread, pearls; silk-screened, image transfer, hand embroidered and pieced ● Collection of Lisa Siders and Dr. Thomas Kenney ● Photo by Pam Braun

Bodil Gardner brings us the pastoral joy of the Danish countryside, while Jenny Bowker celebrates the friends that she made while living in Egypt.

Pat Kumicich, Viola Burley Leak, and Ulva Ugerup use their art to call attention to a variety of political and social issues: Pat looks at the pain caused by war, Viola focuses on African American concerns, and Ulva concentrates on women's rights. Mary Pal's unusual portrait technique shows us the beauty of the elderly, while Joan Sowada focuses on the intensity of children at play. Lori Lupe Pelish shows the pain and uncertainty often present in family life, while Sonia Bardella, Margene May, and Maria Elkins celebrate the love found within families.

Sherry Davis Kleinman and Margot Lovinger present to us the beauty of the human form, though Sherry works with paint and graphite, and Margot uses layer upon layer of sheer overlay. Yoshiko Kurihara and Kathy Nida, each in her own way, explore the human condition: Yoshiko's people are symbols of the passage of time, part of a seemingly endless party. Kathy's subjects symbolize the universal condition of women as mothers and protectors. Pam RuBert's portraits show us the humor in our everyday life, and Carol Goddu invites us all to dance.

As I chose the images for this book, I encountered a few strongly compelling pieces that didn't fit into any of the gallery categories. I wanted to share them here because of their power: once I saw them, I couldn't forget them. Art quilts, like other art forms, often celebrate the incredible complexity of the human condition. Some are created to memorialize tragedies and disasters. Terrie Mangat created *Esme* for her friend Lisa Siders. When Lisa's daughter, Esme, was 13, she was murdered by a man who had been incarcerated for killing several other young women and recently released. Terrie writes, "I put x's through the 'Get out of Jail' cards that I appliquéd down the left-hand side, and I added photos of the other women who had been killed previously in the shadows."

Marilyn Belford's *Medea Escaping* is a powerful example of how an art quilt can bring an ancient tragedy to life. Inspired by Greek mythology, the piece depicts Medea's departure from Corinth after she was betrayed by Jason of the Argonauts. The chariot she rides in was sent by her grandfather, Helios, god of the Sun.

Art quilts can bring a community together. The *Forever Yours* project, organized by Cindy Friedman and the Heartstring Quilters Guild in honor of founding member Jo-Ann Dooley, does just that. Cindy writes, "Jo-Ann made the suggestion that we make a quilt in honor of the rings of people affected by a cancer diagnosis. The images presented are real people whose lives have been touched by cancer, and

MARILYN BELFORD ● MEDEA ESCAPING, 2009 ● 81 1/2 x 102 1/2 inches (207 x 260.4 cm) ● 100% cotton; fused, machine thread sketched, long-arm quilted ● Photo by artist

HEARTSTRING QUILTERS GUILD organized by CYNTHIA D. FRIEDMAN ● FOREVER YOURS, 2011 ● 60 x 90 inches (152.4 x 228.6 cm) ● Silk, silk organza, paint; machine quilted, thread work, fused ● Photo by John Carlano

the blocks were created by various Guild members. Many of them felt it was a cathartic experience to be able to acknowledge someone in their lives who had been affected by cancer and to make a block as a tribute. One woman who had lost her husband to a brain tumor said it was 'like being able to touch his face again' when she was working on his portrait. There is a clear and deep emotional message and commitment in every block."

While I was working on this book, I spent a weekend in New York City. Across the street from my hotel was a row of restaurants: Burrito House, Yawa Sushi, New Shevan Restaurant, Petit Abeille, and Domino's Pizza. The variety of ethnic eateries seemed like the perfect metaphor for the astounding array of people depicted in these pages. If scientists are right, we're all the descendants of one man and one woman and share the same DNA. And yet we come in so very many different sizes, colors, and shapes. Our human family is infinitely varied and unendingly interesting, and—as this book demonstrates—it serves as a rich source of inspiration for artists around the world. I hope that you enjoy meeting the personalities and people portrayed in this collection.

—Martha Sielman

JOAN SOWADA

WHETHER THEY'RE ENGAGED IN SANDBOX PLAY or contemplating the universe, the people in Joan Sowada's work are completely present in the moment, focused on what they're doing. The backgrounds of Sowada's pieces are usually abstracted, so we often can't see what her people are focused upon. We can only share in the intensity of their gaze. Sowada's fused-appliqué technique creates realistic portraits, though a closer look reveals surprising highlights, such as couched yarns that emphasize contours or skin tones that consist of plaids and florals. While admiring the artistry that creates these effects, we remain captivated by the energy of each encapsulated moment.

SPRAY, 2005 ● 16 x 20¹/₂ inches (40.6 x 52.1 cm) ●
Commercial fabrics; fused, machine appliquéd and quilted
● Photo by David Nicholas

Love Affair with Fabric

I have some delightful early memories of kindergarten, when I wore a floppy shirt and painted with giant brushes on newsprint paper at an easel. I still like the spontaneity of paint and use it to create and alter fabrics. Paint, crayons, and markers all have a place in my toolbox, but it's fabric that I love.

I began working with fabric in my early high school years because it was clean, odorless, and unique. I've had a love affair with fabric ever since. It's a medium that provides a huge range of voices while also being tactile and comforting. These qualities are just right for expressing the things I want to say. Fabric is the perfect vehicle.

People as Metaphors

I see each person in my work as a metaphor for other people who have similar characteristics. I find the ways in which we're all the same to be more interesting than the ways in which we're different. My choice

FLIGHT ZONE, 2010 ● 51¹/₂ x 49 inches (129.5 x 124.5 cm) ● Commercial fabrics, oil pastel; fused, machine appliquéd and quilted ● Photo by Ken Sanville

of subject is based on the qualities of composition, mood, light, and shadow. I use a camera to capture the moments that I find compelling. I'm drawn to candid situations that show people in relationships with each other and their environment. I feel I get the best images when people either don't know I'm photographing them or are able to ignore me entirely.

Fabrics

I use the 100% cotton fabrics found at quilt shops. I also purchase hand-dyed cotton fabrics from friends. I've found that linen accepts Setacolor paint in a unique way, so I've been using it in my recent work.

I've stockpiled corduroy and wool but have yet to give them a second life.

I use Setacolor paint to create whole-cloth pieces and to alter the colors of commercial fabrics. These are important additions to my representational pieces. I enjoy using textile paint to make gelatin prints. I do these over commercial fabrics or Setacolor-painted fabrics. I also use oil pastel sticks, textile crayons, and markers.

"Fresh Outlook"

I knew this image would become an art quilt as soon as I saw it. The relaxation and shared experience of the dad and the boys were just right. I liked the

FRESH OUTLOOK, 2006 ● 32 x 43 inches (81.3 x 109.2 cm) ● Commercial and painted fabrics, oil pastel, embroidery floss; fused, machine appliquéd and quilted ● Photo by David Nicholas

BOYS, 2007 ● 27 x 30¹/₂ inches (68.6 x 77.5 cm) ● Commercial fabrics, oil pastel; fused, machine appliquéd and quilted ● Photo by David Nicholas

cropped composition (head and legs out of the frame) and the negative spaces between the figures. The light and shadow were perfect as well. The original photo had a solid, turquoise-blue background, and I thought that it competed with the figures and added nothing. So I created an ambiguous background that was horizontal, which would then support the direction of the railing.

I took the photo to a copy shop to make a paper pattern in the desired size. I made a tracing of the paper pattern and cut a piece of muslin to use as the base for all the fusing. I selected mostly mottled, solid-ish fabrics and decided to go with purple grey and dirty lime as the main background colors. The central shirt color made a nice triad, and everything else was chosen to make these three colors work.

I prepared the fabrics with fusible web. I put the muslin base fabric on a large ironing surface, placed the tracing over it, and weighed it down with beanbags. Lifting the tracing paper in one area at a time, I fused background pieces first, cutting them out freehand without preplanning. I cut up the paper pattern and used these pieces to cut fabric for the railing and the figures. I cut out just a few pieces at a time, fusing fabric bits in one small area before moving on. The tracing helped with the exact placement of the pieces.

I removed the tracing paper and hung up the fused quilt top for a proper look. The tweaking of this piece was largely done with some scribbles of oil pastel on clothing areas and some well-placed tiny bits of pink fabric. Raw-edge appliqué was done with a free-motion foot on my machine, matching thread color to fabrics.

I used the pillowcase system of finishing the edge before doing the quilting. The piece has minimal quilting around the railing and figures and a bit in the top edge and clothing. It has a second outline of the figures a quarter inch outside of the first. I couched white and black embroidery floss in some areas around the figures for even more emphasis of the noodle-like nature of the boys.

When the Art Flows

I focus on one area at a time and try to make the work as interesting as possible. I'm open to what the fabrics want to say. When things are going well, time disappears, and the art flows through me. My dialogue with the medium is effortless. I listen to my gut as I go. If something isn't feeling good, I move to another area. If I'm tired or impatient, I take a break. I give myself time to do some subconscious problem-solving. Energy and fresh eyes make everything easier. If there's an area that I have less confidence about, I save it for last. Close to the end, the fabric choices seem more obvious and flow easily.

I don't really see the work overall until the tissue paper comes off. Then I like to look at it upside down and sideways, in low light and from a distance. Usually any problems I see are due to something being too weak or too strong. These problems can be fixed. I call this stage of the process "tweaking," and it's my favorite time! I like that small changes can have a huge impact. Sometimes it's the quilting or a border that brings it all together.

FLOW, 2007 ● 11 x 27 inches (27.9 x 68.6 cm) ● Commercial fabrics, embroidery floss; fused, machine appliquéd and quilted ● Photo by David Nicholas

SIBLING DUET, 2009 ● 33 x 30 inches (83.8 x 76.2 cm) ● Commercial fabrics, paint, markers; fused, machine appliquéd and quilted ● Photo by Ken Sanville

BODIL GARDNER

THE SUN IS ALWAYS SHINING IN BODIL GARNDER'S WORLDS. The skies are blue, and the grass is green. Sheep cavort in the meadows. Round, rosy cheeks, quirky smiles, and off-kilter eyes give her figures a tremendous sense of fun and exuberance. Begun as a way to decorate the mended patches on her children's clothing, Gardner's work is still driven by a sense that each picture should be created out of whatever fabrics she has on hand so as not to waste material. Gardner finds this limitation of her palette artistically liberating. Her cheerful inhabitants of the Danish countryside invite us to join them in a world of peace and abundance.

LADY WITH LEMONS, 2008 ● 29 x 29 inches (73.7 x 73.7 cm) ● Recycled cottons; raw-edge appliquéd, machine quilted ● Photo by Peter Gardner

Becoming an Artist

In my youth, I never imagined that I could be anything but practical. My father and my sister, both of whom painted, were the creative members of my family. My father was a member of a committee in charge of choosing and buying art for local schools, so I spent many a weekend visiting artists and art galleries. I quickly learned what a good painting was and realized my own limitations.

While I was at school, I promised myself that when I became old enough to make my own decisions, I would never have a needle in my hand except to sew on a button. Needlework at school was awful. However, for a housewife with four children, it turned out to be a necessity. I bought a sewing machine and began making my children's clothes, and I soon found that I was decorating them to cover up holes and alterations. One day, I needed a new bedspread and had enough leftover material to make it. That was the start—still practical.

After many bedspreads—composites made from small pictures pieced together—I suddenly had the urge to make a picture for its own sake. Now it's as though I paint with my material, and stopping seems impossible. There's a type of freedom in sewing pictures instead of painting them. If I painted, I'd be forced to

JOURNEYS END IN LOVERS MEETING, 2009 ● 52 x 39 inches (132.1 x 99.1 cm) ● Recycled cottons; raw-edge appliquéd, machine quilted ● Photo by Peter Gardner

mix my colors to obtain the "correct" hues, whereas now I find out what I have, and that's what I use. In fact, there are no rules and no expectations.

Not Being Afraid

The most challenging aspect of working in fiber is making use of the material I have instead of buying new fabric. I have to not be afraid of using a piece of green material when I'd intended to make a figure with yellow hair. I use the fabric as it is, including the reverse side if that looks more like what I need. Once or twice I've had to dye a fabric to get the right blue for the sky. I can always alter a not-quite-satisfactory color by means of the sewing thread I use. I must admit that once in a while I think about painting. At present, it's difficult to find really good yellows and greens—colors that vibrate.

Danish Countryside

I usually try to tell a story. I grew up in Copenhagen, but my father's family were farmers near the west coast of Denmark. As a child, I was sent there for months at a time because of illness in the family, and I also spent my summer holidays there. My parents

ORGANIC IS GOOD FOR YOU, 2011 ● 55 x 52 inches (139.7 x 132.1 cm) ● Recycled cottons; raw-edge appliquéd, machine quilted ● Photo by Peter Gardner

SHOW ME THE ROAD TO TIMBUKTU, 2009 ● 44 x 41 inches (111.8 x 104.1 cm) ●
Recycled cottons; raw-edge appliquéd, machine quilted ● Photo by Peter Gardner

had the idea that children should know their own country before going abroad, and they cycled through Denmark for a fortnight every summer with my sister and me, a practice my husband and I repeated with our four children. So I know the Danish countryside and landscape pretty well. Its green softness gives me a feeling of freedom.

I use sheep in almost every piece. As a child on holiday, one of my farming uncles always had a lamb we fed with a bottle. In 2004, while walking on the Berkshire Downs, I saw how much the scattered sheep contributed to the look of the English landscape—specks of white on the green. Since then, I've used sheep as a way of getting white into a picture.

I like having them emphasize the curves in a landscape. They're visually attractive and lend a feeling of innocence.

Coffee Cups

The coffee cup is my symbol for women getting together and sharing—perhaps even solving—their problems. Men share a beer, while women tend to bond over a cup of tea or coffee. Having a cup in your hand means you don't have to look anyone in the face—you can concentrate on the cup and find it easier to talk. So the cup is both a symbol of woman-hood and an invitation.

DREAMING OF YOU, 2009 ● 39 x 38 inches (99.1 x 96.5 cm) ● Recycled cottons; raw-edge appliquéd, machine quilted ● Photo by Peter Gardner

Experimental Process

I never draw. When I lie awake at night, I plan pictures in my head—the broad outlines, no ready-made designs! As soon as I know what my picture will consist of, I search through my stock of fabrics for the right colors in the right materials and sizes. The whole picture is built up on a double layer of sheet or curtain material in keeping with my principle of recycling whatever I have. I build up the background on top of this, followed by the person who will be the focus point.

I don't design so much as experiment, moving things around and allowing the picture to develop itself as

I discover new possibilities, often in bits of fabric, which look and feel right "just there." Finally, I fill out the background.

I kneel on the floor as I work, keeping everything in place with lots of pins. I don't use any other fixative mechanisms. Walking around the piece, I regard it from all angles and very often find things to change. Days pass, maybe a week or two, with me just looking, and then I start sewing. At this stage, the design is fixed—or very difficult to alter.

I always try to start sewing in the middle of the piece. I often stop to reset the pins and smooth things out.

DREAM HOUSES, 2007 ● 39 x 39 inches (99.1 x 99.1 cm) ● Recycled cottons; raw-edge appliquéd, machine quilted ● Photo by Peter Gardner

I use raw-edge appliqué, so the color of the thread plays an important role. In addition to fastening down the edges and layers of material, I sometimes need to emphasize the edges by using contrasting colors or have them disappear by using a matching color. I may also use zigzag stitching to draw in details.

Creative Satisfaction

I'd like viewers to sense the simplicity and innocence in my pictures. For me it's the happiness of making them that counts, not trying to impress others. I'm trying to create something that makes me happy. I am, generally speaking, a very optimistic person who tries to get the best out of every situation. I think my choice of colors creates an illusion of something good and pleasant in my pictures.

I'm glad when people like my work, but that's not my main purpose. My aim has always been to encourage others to be creative, to feel the satisfaction of having produced something original. When I make pictures, I forget my worries and sometimes laugh to myself. I want to pass that experience on to others!

MARIA ELKINS

YOU NEVER KNOW WHAT YOU'LL SEE NEXT when you view works by Maria Elkins. A frequent experimenter, she enjoys trying new techniques and approaches. Though many of Elkins' contemporary portraits contain references to traditional quilt block patterns, her techniques are anything but traditional: sheers, inks, paintsticks, unusual use of space, and intense machine quilting all find a place in her work. Elkins depends on family and friends to model for her, cajoling them into poses that capture the essence of childhood and family memories. While her methods continually change, it's clear that her love for the process remains the same.

EVENING STAR, 2002 ● 39 x 31 inches (99.1 x 78.7 cm)
● 100% cotton, paint; hand pieced and quilted ●
Photo by artist

Family as Models

I portray people I know—people who are close to me emotionally. I also ask people to model whom I know won't say no. I shamelessly exploit my two sweet daughters. One loves to have her picture taken, so I use her quite frequently; the other isn't thrilled about being photographed but is still a willing subject. Sometimes I end up doing self-portraits because I'm always available!

For *Broken Dishes*, I asked a friend and her daughter—a beautiful little blonde girl with a flair for the dramatic—to pose. I told the little girl that I wanted to take a picture of someone who had just broken a plate and whose mommy was hugging her. Once she understood she wasn't in trouble, she threw herself into the part.

Okay to Fail

I now tend to approach art as one big experiment, and I love to try new products and techniques. For many years I wanted to take this approach but a fear of failure always held me back. Then, in 2002, Karey Bresenhan, CEO of Quilts, Inc., spearheaded the Journal Quilt project. The idea was to create an 8½ x 11-inch (21.5 x 27.9 cm) quilt each month for nine months.

BROKEN DISHES, 2009 ● 58 x 42 inches (147.3 x 106.7 cm) ● 100% cotton, silk organza, textile paint, paintsticks; fused appliqué, machine quilted ● Photo by artist

The small format was chosen to encourage people to experiment. I wanted to explore different mediums on both cotton and silk, so I divided my little quilts vertically and placed silk on the left and cotton on the right. Each month, I used a different product: crayons, colored pencils, paintsticks, ink, paints,

and dye. I also tried a different thread and a different embellishment on each piece.

These experiments showed me that it's okay to fail. This has helped me to move forward with less fear. Now I make it a goal to work with various mediums. Each offers me a different way of saying something,

FLIGHT OF FANCY, 2003   ●   40 x 40 inches (101.6 x 101.6 cm)   ●   100% cotton, textile paint, ink, pens; fused appliqué, machine quilted   ●   Photo by artist

so I consider each new image before choosing the medium. I remind myself each time that it's just a piece of fabric. If I don't like it, I can throw it away. This makes the project much less stressful, so I can just enjoy the creative process.

The Process for "Windblown"

For *Windblown*, I wanted to create a quilt with the look and feel of a watercolor painting. The quilt ended up taking a different direction, but that's part of the adventure of experimenting. I started by taking a wide variety of photographs of my model. She's one of my daughters' friends, and I've always loved her long, wavy hair and sweet, gentle face. She patiently put up with a strong wind that hopelessly tangled her hair, while I took more than a hundred pictures.

I transferred all of the photos to my computer, identified elements that I liked, and combined several images. Then I drew the resulting image full-size on paper. When I was happy with the image, I transferred it to Pimatex cotton using a fabric gel pen. I used this piece to experiment with a new way of painting using Tsukineko All-Purpose Inks. I first tried a watercolor approach, but I wasn't at all pleased with my results, so I started again with a fresh piece of fabric. This time, I mixed the ink with a thickener and painted the image. It didn't give me quite the watercolor-painting type of result I'd originally imagined, but I was pleased enough with the image to continue.

WINDBLOWN, 2011 ● 25 x 39 inches (63.5 x 99.1 cm) ● 100% cotton, all-purpose ink; machine quilted ● Photo by artist

SHEER WHIM, 2010 ● 17 x 17 inches (43.2 x 43.2 cm) ● 100% cotton, sheer fabrics, fabric crayons, paintstiks, all-purpose ink; machine quilted ● Photo by artist

Once the main figure was painted, I took a photograph of the painted fabric and opened it in my digital editing program so I could audition various backgrounds. I was particularly interested in choosing a background color and intensity that would push the image forward and complement the model's hair color. I ended up painting the background with a stipple brush to create a soft effect in the sky.

After the quilt top was completely painted, I thought about possible quilting lines. I wanted to capture the feeling of the wind in the piece. I also love traditional quilted feather motifs, so I wondered if I could somehow combine the two ideas. I have often included traditional quilt blocks in my work, and I wanted to include one in this piece. I thought the angular shapes in a traditional block would contrast nicely with all of the curvy lines of the image. I used Barbara Brackman's *Encyclopedia of Pieced Quilt Patterns* to research various blocks that might have "wind" or "storm" or some similar word in their names. I ended up quilting the outline of the "Windblown Star" blocks in the sky among the wind gusts. I enhanced parts of the block and some strands of hair with Shiva Paintstiks to add some texture and shimmer.

After I finished drawing my quilting lines on tracing paper, I transferred the main lines to my quilt top using a dissolving stabilizer and began freemotion quilting. I used mostly 40-weight polyester thread, except on the face and hand, where I used 100-weight silk threads. At the end, I added a few metallic threads in her hair and in the sky.

Challenges of Quilting

I think quilting portraits may be one of the most difficult aspects of my work. I've spent most of my life building a strong foundation in drawing and sewing, so I feel reasonably confident in those two areas. When it comes to actually quilting a piece, though, the process can be stressful. The quilting lines can enhance what's already there, or they can create a disaster.

Because my free-motion quilting stitches are typically small, it's particularly difficult to tear out unsuccessful quilting lines, so that creates additional pressure to do it right the first time. As a result, quilting seems to be the biggest risk for me. I try to spend significant time auditioning my thread options first and sketching out possible stitching lines. Then I take a deep breath and try to think brave thoughts!

Positive Messages

I want to create quilts that convey positive messages, quilts that are beautiful and make viewers smile. If my work stirs fond memories or encourages them in some way, that's even better.

I want to create images that people will remember. For instance, it's satisfying to hear someone tell me they remember seeing *Wedding Dreams* or *Stolen Lives*, both made in 2001. To me, that means those quilts were successful and they did their job. It doesn't bother me to hear someone say, "I didn't know you made that quilt." I'm actually more surprised when people know my name!

STOLEN LIVES, 2001 ● 28 x 18 inches (71.1 x 45.7 cm) ● 100% cotton, textile paint, pen; inkjet printed, fused appliqué, machine quilted ● Photo by artist

happiness

JO-ANN GOLENIA ● WAYNE, 2009 ● 25^1/$_4$ x 25^1/$_4$ inches (64.1 x 64.1 cm) ● 100% cotton fabric, batting, thread; raw-edge machine appliquéd, machine quilted ● Photo by artist

DENISE TALLON HAVLAN ● SNAPSHOT: SHANNON'S BANTAM, 2009 ● 63 x 45 inches (160 x 114.3 cm) ●
Cotton, paint, ink; hand and machine appliquéd, machine quilted and embroidered ● Photo by artist

YOKO SEKITA ● GREAT DAY TO BE BUSY!, 2009 ● 74 x 59 x $^1/_2$ inches (188 x 149.9 x 1.3 cm) ●
Cotton, silk, wool; hand pieced and quilted ● Photo by Yasuyuki Sekita

PHYLLIS A. CULLEN ● LOVEBIRDS, 2009
● 22 x 27 inches (55.9 x 68.6 cm) ●
Commercial and hand-dyed cotton, paint;
raw-edge collage, machine quilted
● Photo by artist

MAGGIE DILLON ● SISTERS AT SELBY, 2011
● 48 x 42 inches (121.9 x 106.7 cm) ●
Batik fabric; thread work, machine appliquéd
● Photo by artist

VIRGINIA GREAVES ● CELTIC WOMAN, 2010 ● 24 x 20 inches (61 x 50.8 cm) ● 100% cotton; machine appliquéd and quilted ● Photo by artist

HOLLY HASCALL DOMINIE ● IRREPRESSIBLE, 2010 ● 38 x 27 1/2 inches (96.5 x 69.9 cm) ●
100% cotton, glue; fabric collage, machine quilted ● Photo by Tom Way

MARILYN H. WALL ● CONNOR, 2011 ● 32¹/₂ x 27¹/₂ inches (82.6 x 69.9 cm) ● 100% cotton; hand dyed, raw-edge appliquéd, thread painted, free-motion machine quilted ● Photo by G. Lee Wall

GRACE JOAN ERREA ● LOVE AT FIRST SIGHT, 2009 ● 25 x 31 inches (63.5 x 78.7 cm) ● 100% cotton, machine appliquéd and quilted ● Photo by Dan Snipes Photography

CINDI LYNNE GREENE ● GRANDMA'S JOY, 2009 ● 8 x 10 inches (20.3 x 25.4 cm) ● 100% muslin cotton, cotton and polyester fabric remnants, photo template, fusible web, thread ● Photo by Brea Greene

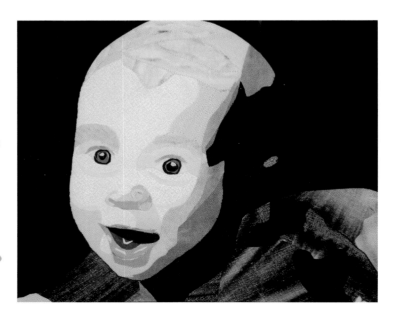

COLETTE BERENDS

THE GLOWING COLORS IN COLETTE BERENDS' PORTRAITS conjure up visions of romance and elegance, of lives filled with gaiety and despair. The vignettes so captivate us that we have to concentrate carefully in order to see the fabrics from which they are created. Each wall hanging is made of hundreds of tiny fabric pieces appliquéd together. Overlays of netting create shadows and texture. Glittery fabrics add highlights. Threads and yarns emphasize important details. A lifelong fan of the circus, the theater, and the movies, Berends passed away before this book was published but her work draws us into a world where life is lived to the fullest with intensity and passion.

LULLABY, 2004 ● 19^{11}/$_{16}$ x 27^{9}/$_{16}$ inches (50 x 70 cm) ● Silk, wool, cotton, mixed media, lace, leather, yarns, heavy crêpe de chine, silk paints; hand quilted ● Photo by artist

Fiber Is More Expressive

Fiber is so much more expressive than paint. If I were to place my fiber work next to a painting, the painting would look faded. Also, there's such a variety of textures and colors available in fiber, and these effects can never be achieved with paint.

Fabric is much more expensive than paint, but the color is stronger and has a glow. Of course, working with fiber is not so far removed from painting; you use the same principles. A painter is trying to express something on a canvas. I try to achieve that with fabric. Fabric is probably more difficult to work with than paint. Fabric is concrete—you use that piece, and that is it. With a paintbrush you can change an image somewhat, letting it fade or changing the effect.

Previous Careers

One of my first careers was as a shop-window designer. I enjoyed working with fabrics and colors to create designs. I then had a lengthy career as a nightclub entertainer. I traveled all over the world. In India, I slept in the palace of the Maharaja shortly after independence. I experienced floating restaurants in Hong Kong and drag shows in Singapore. I was enraptured by the temple dances of Bali, and I

AUTUMN LEAVES, 2006 ● 39³/₈ x 23⁵/₈ inches (100 x 60 cm) ● Silk, wool, cotton, mixed media, lace, leather, yarns, heavy crêpe de chine, silk paints; hand quilted ● Photo by artist

PARTY, 2000 ● 43⁵/₁₆ x 25⁹/₁₆ inches (110 x 65 cm) ● Silk, wool, cotton, mixed media, lace, leather, yarns, heavy crêpe de chine, silk paints; hand quilted ● Photo by artist

slept in long-houses in the jungles of Borneo. I traveled across South America and the United States and cruised throughout northern Europe, the Mediterranean, and the Greek islands.

When I retired from being an entertainer, I opened a beauty salon in my hometown of Zwolle. I was no longer traveling, and I wanted to do something that would make me happy for the rest of my days. I'd had a very exciting life, and suddenly I was stuck between four walls in an apartment. I needed to do something, or I was going to go nuts. I'd always loved beautiful fabrics and wanted to create something with them.

Inspiration and Music

My subjects come from the cinema, nightclubs, romantic theater, ballet, and the circus. They come from the love between a husband and a wife or a mother and a child. I've never had children, but I can understand what it means to be a mother. Music is very important to me. I listen often, especially while working, to deepen the process. My work is a bit auto-biographical, but viewers shouldn't dig too deeply for meaning.

Beautiful Materials

I don't consciously try to use a particular palette. The inspiration of the moment guides me. If I'm repeating myself, so be it. There are incredible quantities of color in my work. And beautiful materials! Frank Govers and Rob Kröner, both Dutch designers of *haute couture*, give me leftover pieces of their materials, often very small pieces, but I don't need large quantities.

I do shop around to find the material I need for a particular work. I frequently visit flea markets and antique stores in my hunt for special bits and pieces. I find materials there that are no longer available. I don't dye or paint the fabrics I use. The only exception is the old lace that I buy at antique fairs. Since it tends to be faded by the years, I do color it.

I use all kinds of fabrics: silk, wool, cotton, and everything in between, including lace, leather, and metal. My works are composed of hundreds of tiny pieces of fabric. To give you an example: in *Mother and Child*, a relatively small canvas that's 11½ x 14½ inches (29 x 37 cm), I used more than 300 pieces of fabric.

TANGO, 2009 ● 45¼ x 27⁹/₁₆ inches (115 x 70 cm) ● Silk, wool, cotton, mixed media, lace, leather, yarns, heavy crêpe de chine, silk paints; hand quilted ● Photo by artist

MOTHER, 2008 ● 26³/₄ x 20⁷/₈ inches (68 x 53 cm) ● Silk, wool, cotton, mixed media, lace, leather, yarns, heavy crêpe de chine, silk paints; hand quilted ● Photo by artist

All Handmade

I do everything by hand. I start by making drawings on transparent paper, varying the scale of all the models I think I'll use. By layering them one over the other, I'm able to see the whole composition. Once I'm pleased with the composition, I place the drawing under white silk (heavy crêpe de chine) that's been stretched in a frame. I can see through the silk to draw my sketch onto the silk base.

I use silk paints right out of the tube to outline my designs and fill in the basic colors of the design. I make the paint permanent with eight hours of steaming. I wash the silk to get it smooth and clean, line it with cotton for strength, and cut it to the right size. Finally, I mount the entire thing on jute. Then I fix it onto hardboard and—like a painter—put it upright on a painter's easel. Working with it upright allows me to view it better than when it's flat on the table.

Next, I pin pieces of fabric to make my concept complete. I pin a first layer to the background, then a second, and a third. Each layer contributes to a richer, many-hued whole. If I'm working with expensive fabric, I make a paper stencil first and position it carefully to find the most advantageous layout before cutting.

I spend a lot of time with the faces. Mouths and eyes I cut directly with scissors. Then I try them this way and that way until they're proportioned just right. I fasten them to the background with thread that I use very deliberately. This thread functions like a brushstroke or a pencil line. I use it to create wrinkles in a face or add contour to an eye. Finally, I hang the picture on my wall for a while to see if the composition is indeed right.

A wall hanging takes hundreds of hours. It's important that the composition is right, and that a certain balance is achieved. Otherwise, a piece can become messy because there are too many colors.

PAT KUMICICH

IF "THE PERSONAL IS POLITICAL," THEN ONE OF THE PLACES that this insight is best expressed is Pat Kumicich's artwork. Frequently using herself as a model, Kumicich examines a variety of social and political themes: women's body-image issues, the intersection of war and politics, the tragedy of domestic violence. Her skillful photo-image transfers create backgrounds for her figures that are full of intriguing commentary. Many of Kumicich's portraits convey powerful emotions. Her feelings of pain at the resumption of armed hostilities are so apparent in one portrait that the viewer hardly notices how her face is constructed from two clashing colors.

HMMM..., 2008 ● 51 x 51 inches (129.5 x 129.5 cm) ●
100% cotton, paint, embroidery floss, tulle; inkjet printed,
machine pieced, appliquéd, and quilted, hand embroidered
● Photo by artist

Fabric Has Given Me a Voice

Like many artists throughout history, I find it difficult to articulate my feelings in a conventional way. Fabric has given me a voice, allowing me to create colorful, powerful statements about the things that I love or find abhorrent or am moved by. I'm often inspired by women in the news and by women I know or imagine. They're reflected in the strong textures, vibrant colors, and wide variety of fabrics and threads that characterize my work.

I find politics to be fascinating. I admire people who take a stand on principle. From my perspective, mixing politics with art is natural. I use war as a theme because it's part of my life. My husband served in the U.S. Army in Vietnam. My son is a Marine who served in Panama and participated in Operation Desert Storm. I know that others think of war as a necessary evil, but I hope that one day we can learn to resolve our differences through peaceful means.

Art Is Autobiographical

My biggest challenge in creating art is figuring out a way to represent my emotions. I'm basically a happy person, but my quilts tend to lean towards the dark

NO END IN SIGHT, 2008 ● 39 x 49 inches (99.1 x 124.5 cm) ● 100% cotton, silk, silk organza, paint, embroidery floss; inkjet printed, hand embroidered, machine pieced, appliquéd, and quilted ● Photo by artist

side. Since most of my pieces are autobiographical, I often use photos of myself. I either set up my camera on a tripod and use a timer or have my husband take pictures of me while I pose. I use the photographs as references for creating my drawings.

I like to draw. I often start with a doodle or quick sketch, then decide on the size of the finished quilt and enlarge the sketch by hand. I tend to work intuitively. Using a computer would seem too much like work—at least for me! I like getting my hands dirty.

The backgrounds help pull my compositions together. I often use image transfers to print photos onto the fabric. For instance, the background of *Weight,*

Weight—Don't Tell Me! is comprised of rear-end views of women and various articles about weight and weight loss. The background creates an additional layer of interest, drawing the viewer in to take a closer look.

Making Do

I enjoy the challenge of "making do" with the materials I have on hand. I rarely buy fabric for a specific project. I like the challenge of painting and/or dyeing fabrics or using alternate fibers, such as paper, felt, or yarn, before deciding which materials will work best in what I'm trying to communicate to the viewer.

WEIGHT, WEIGHT—DON'T TELL ME!, 2010 ● 54 x 42 inches (137.2 x 106.7 cm) ● 100% cotton, paint, buttons, beads, found objects, lace, embroidery floss; machine pieced, appliquéd, and quilted, inkjet printed, hand embroidered ● Photo by artist

GOSSIP GIRLS, 2011 ● 47 x 47 inches (119.4 x 119.4 cm) ●
100% cotton, silk, synthetic fabric, cheesecloth, paper, paint,
ink, beads, embroidery floss; machine pieced and quilted,
hand embroidered, image transfer, laminated ●
Photo by artist

SHOULD I?, 2009 ● 49$^{1}/_{2}$ x 49$^{1}/_{2}$ inches (125.8 x 125.8 cm)
● 100% cotton, tulle, paint, embroidery floss; inkjet printed,
machine pieced, appliquéd, and quilted, hand embroidered
● Photo by artist

Experimenting with different techniques is an integral part of my art. I dye, paint, or print many of the fabrics I use and often incorporate found objects. Items that have been discarded as no longer useful find new life in my quilts.

Start with the Title

I start with an idea: I find it helpful to have a title in mind from the beginning because this keeps me focused. I then create a variety of preliminary photographs, doodles, and sketches. Once I find a composition that I like, I determine the finished size of the piece, enlarge my drawing to that size, and clean up the drawing, removing any unnecessary components. I decide which techniques to use after my drawing is complete. My drawings are like puzzle pieces. Once the drawing is finished, I can best determine the easiest, most efficient way to put it together.

I number the individual components and mark the drawing with registration or directional marks. If the quilt is going to be predominantly pieced, I next transfer the drawing onto fusible interfacing. I transfer the numbers and registration marks, etc. Then I cut the pieces of the drawing out.

I choose my colors and fabrics next. I make lots of small samples—color, thread, stitching. It's easier for me to work this way, with less waste of time and materials. Once my drawing is complete and I've chosen or made the fabrics, I'm relatively sure that the piece will go well.

Then I make a list of the component parts, attaching a swatch of fabric to the list for each component piece. I prepare the fabrics—I dye, paint, laminate, and print, if necessary—and adhere interfacing to the fabrics. When I cut out the shapes, I leave a generous seam allowance. The various elements are prepared separately. As I work, I decide on placement and baste any turn-under seams. I use monofilament thread and a zigzag stitch to join the elements together.

Sometimes I piece the entire quilt top; other times, I add hand or machine appliqué. I don't do much traditional hand quilting, but I do like the texture of hand quilting with heavy threads, so I use, for lack of a better description, a stab stitch—usually three or four strands of embroidery floss or a single strand of size 8 perle cotton thread. Free-motion quilting is another option that I use often. I make those

NO NEWS IS GOOD NEWS, 2006 ● 51 x 51 inches (129.5 x 129.5 cm) ● Silk, silk organza, paint; inkjet printed, machine and hand appliquéd, machine pieced and quilted, stenciled ● Photo by artist

decisions once the top is complete, sometimes combining both hand and machine quilting for added interest and texture.

Food for Thought

I love making my mark with needle and thread. I'm gratified if the viewer takes the time to study one of my pieces. I'm always hopeful that my work is food for thought.

Over the last several years, my work has been predominantly autobiographical. I hope viewers can relate to how I feel about a particular subject—and then either agree or disagree. Working in the art-quilt medium allows me to express my innermost feelings about our world, the times we live in, and the human condition.

SHERRY DAVIS KLEINMAN

THE SUBJECTS OF SHERRY DAVIS KLEINMAN'S PORTRAITS are very real people: they have wide hips, big thighs, and wrinkles like the rest of us. They sit quietly contemplating life, their thoughts unknown. Kleinman is a frequent experimenter who uses a variety of techniques and media, including appliqué, painting, and graphite drawing, sometimes separately and sometimes in combination. Even Kleinman's public scenes have an intimacy to them: we're privileged to share a fleeting glimpse into her subjects' inner lives.

DATE NIGHT AT THE DRIVE-IN, 2009 ● 30 x 23 inches (76.2 x 58.4 cm) ● Raw cotton canvas, crayons, colored pencils, whole cloth, cotton batting, buttons; machine and hand stitched ● Photo by Steven Kleinman

Rip Van Winkle

I've been interested in doing portraits for as long as I can remember. Faces are fascinating to me: young or old, homely or beautiful, everyone is different. As a teenager, I spent hours copying photos I found in magazines and newspapers. However, when I entered college I didn't feel confident enough to major in art and instead majored in history. I've since compensated for that mistake by enrolling in one art class after another.

When my third and youngest daughter left home for art school, I wanted to fill my "empty nest" with something just for me. I hadn't sewn in many years, but my passion for fabric and textures was itching to come out. I treated myself to a new sewing machine and found the world of textiles had changed. I felt like Rip Van Winkle, awakening to rotary cutters and cutting mats and sewing machines that actually worked well.

One day, in the weekly life-drawing class I attend, I tried drawing the figure on fabric instead of paper. WOW! What a change that made in my artistic journey! New possibilities mushroomed daily in my head. I often awoke in the middle of the night with an image in mind that I wanted to create.

MALIBU BEACH, 2011 ● 32 x 29 inches (81.3 x 73.7 cm) ● Canvas, cotton, tulle, water-soluble crayons and pencils; machine pieced and quilted ● Photo by Steven Kleinman

BEDTIME STORIES, 2010 ● 36 x 28 inches (91.4 x 71.1 cm) ● 100% cotton, commercial cottons, cotton and wool batting; fused and machine appliquéd ● Photo by Steven Kleinman

Real Models

In my life-drawing class, we have both nude and clothed models who do two- or three-week poses. I work from a large variety of models. Like the general public, these models are not all Hollywood glamour types. The feedback about the portraits I've created from these models has been very positive. I think that people with wrinkles, curves, and unusual features are more interesting to look at than people who are "perfect." For example, my recent piece, *Malibu Beach*, created a lot of conversation with the viewers at the Long Beach International Quilt Festival. Viewers seemed to love the fact that the portrait was so real, that I didn't present an unrealistic image of beauty.

A Variety of Techniques

Most of my recent work is painted, but I do still love the feel of fabrics. There's no substitute for the fun of auditioning, cutting, appliquéing, and machine stitching fabrics in a collage fashion to create a portrait. My piece *Bedtime Stories* is a reflection of that technique. I did a pencil sketch first, then cut fabrics to create my figures and machine appliquéd them. I even had my husband "model" for me so that I could the right perspective with the feet.

I love to experiment with my materials. I think that's one of the best things about today's art quilts. Anything is possible with fabric; you're only limited by your imagination. Some approaches work and others don't. My sewing-machine repair guy wasn't happy with me when I was in my gesso phase! I experimented with different kinds of fabric, used too many layers of batting, broke needles, shredded threads, and tried this paint and that ink before I found what works best for me.

I currently work on raw painter's canvas, applying a mixture of media to it along with lots of machine stitching. I like to use media that doesn't change the hand of the fabric too much. Painter's canvas has a great heavy weight that really takes well to paint, water, and stitch. Plus I like its texture, which really shows up well in the completed piece.

My favorite media are water-soluble. Currently, I use crayons, colored pencils, and airbrush paint without the airbrush. Airbrush paint is thin and easy to brush onto large areas of color as a base for the crayons and pencils. The colors are rich and vibrant. I also like to use water-soluble graphite pencils for those moments when I need black and white.

"Geisha"

My inspiration for *Geisha* was a vintage, copyright-free photo from the Internet. I stitched meander machine stitching all over a raw canvas fabric, then used an overhead projector to project the photo onto the raw canvas base to get the general size proportions. I painted the image using airbrush paint applied with a paintbrush and water: light green for the background and yellow for the figure and the floor. Then, using water-soluble crayons/pencils, I drew and painted the figure. This process created multiple layers of color, and I liked the intensity and blending I was able to get with the addition of water and more color.

GEISHA, 2011 ● 60 x 24 inches (152.4 x 61 cm) ● Whole-cloth canvas, airbrush paint, crayons, colored pencil, commercial cottons, Japanese silks, cotton batting; machine appliquéd and quilted ● Photo by Steven Kleinman

REHEARSAL, 2008 ● 36 x 20 inches (91.4 x 50.8 cm) ●
Raw cotton canvas and commercial fabrics, cotton batting,
beads; drawn, machine and fused appliqué ● Photo by
Steven Kleinman

During the process of doing the figure, I auditioned the fabrics that I would use to frame it. I wanted to create a Japanese flavor, so I researched Japanese art panels and screens. Using the complementary color of turquoise to offset the oranges and reds of the kimono, I created a curtain-like side border to go with the top and bottom panels. I wanted the viewer to have the feeling of looking into the geisha's private chamber and catching a moment of her beauty ritual.

With the prepared fabric panels set to the side, I returned to the figure. I made a quilt sandwich by adding batting to the canvas (I didn't add backing at this point because I fuse it to the back as my last step before binding). I then added machine quilting to the figure. This is the fun step, when I use thread to enhance the image. I don't do a complete coverage with thread because I want my painting to show through. I like that there are layers of stitching that make for a more complex surface.

Then I added the fabric panels to the central, whole-cloth painting. I machine appliquéd flowers and stick ornaments in the geisha's hair. The hair ornaments are like mini-quilts in that they have batting and were stitched prior to application in the figure's hair. Finally, I fused the backing fabric to the stitched front, squared and trimmed the edges, and added a binding.

Touch a Chord

I'm an observer of people. I like to sit in the back when I'm in a large crowd, so I can see the whole room. I do more listening than talking when in a group. It can be entertaining to watch people you don't know, to imagine what they might be like. When I make a portrait, I have the opportunity to interpret people in my own way.

At shows, in addition to introducing myself, I like to listen to people's comments as they view my work. I love to hear what they think. I guess it's a validation for me that with my work I can touch people in some positive way. It's impossible to please everyone, and I don't expect that, but as an artist I want to reach people. I want my work to have meaning for viewers. I want to touch a chord, provoke a memory, make people linger for a second look.

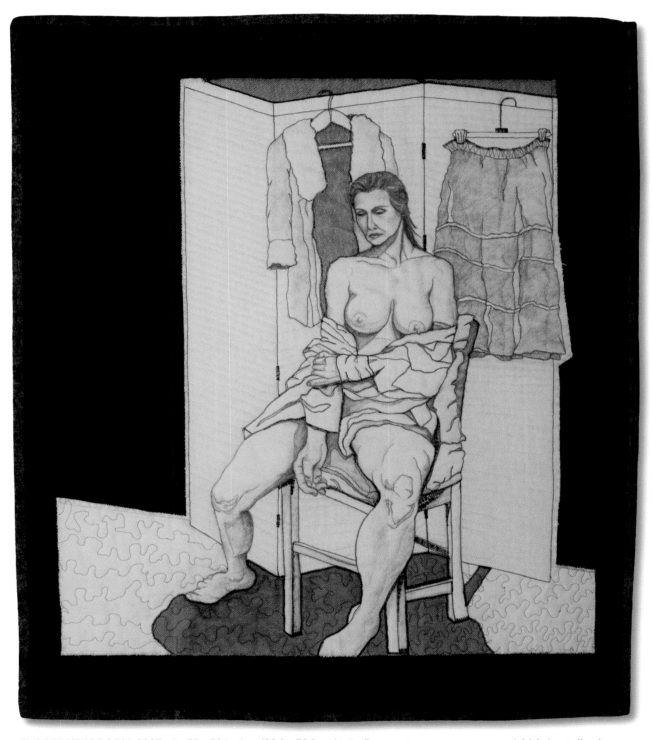

THE DRESSING ROOM, 2007 ● 35 x 30 inches (88.9 x 76.2 cm) ● Raw cotton canvas, commercial fabrics, tulle; drawn, machine stitched ● Photo by Steven Kleinman

contemplation

ANIKO FEHER ● KATI, 2009 ● 26 x 26 inches (66 x 66 cm) ● 100% cotton, watercolor pencil; raw-edge appliquéd, machine quilted ● Photo by artist

JENNIFER ELLEN DAY ● ABUELA, 2010 ● 48 x 41 x ¹/₂ inches (121.9 x 104.1 x 1.3 cm) ● Digitally transferred image, thread; free-motion embroidered ● Photo by High Desert Arts

JYLIAN GUSTLIN ● STAR-CROSSED, 2010 ● 54 x 54 x ¹/₄ inches (137.2 x 137.2 x 0.6 cm) ● Upholstery fabrics, paint, digital images; stitched ● Photo by artist

DEIDRE SCHERER ● IN THOUGHT, 2010 ● 10 x 9 inches
(25.4 x 22.9 cm) ● Cotton, cotton thread; cut, layered, machine
sewn ● Photo by artist

KATE THEMEL ● KATE AT 40, 2010 ●
20 x 21 inches (50.8 x 53.3 cm) ● Cotton fabric, rayon
thread; raw-edge appliquéd, machine stitched and quilted
● Photo by artist

PAMELA PRICE KLEBAUM ● SKETCH, 2011 ●
34 x 15^1/$_2$ inches (86.4 x 39.4 cm) ● Cotton, cotton
sateen, pigment ink, cotton and monofilament
thread, original sketch; digitally painted ● Photo
by artist

SUE KING ● GRAPES OF WRATH, 2011
● 28 x 36 inches (71.1 x 91.4 cm) ●
100% cotton, vintage fabrics; hand dyed,
machine pieced and free-motion quilted
● Photo by Robert Colgan

JULIE DUSCHACK ● MONK IN THE DOORWAY, 2010 ● 49 x 72 x 1 inches (124.5 x 182.9 x 2.5 cm) ●
Commercial cottons and silks, polyester, oil sticks, tulle, beads; hand dyed, over dyed, reverse machine appliquéd,
pieced, thread painted ● Photo by artist

MARY RUTH SMITH ● OUR INDEPENDENCE, 2011 ●
10 x 10³/₄ inches (25.4 x 27.3 cm) ● Silk fabric, newspaper,
matte medium, thread; laminated, hand stitched ●
Photo by Sondra Brady

SHERRI CULVER ● WAITING, 2010 ●
38 x 23 inches (96.5 x 58.4 cm) ● 100% cotton; machine
appliquéd and quilted ● Photo by artist

RANDALL SCOTT COOK ● I REMAIN, 2007
● 81 x 55 inches (205.7 x 139.7 cm) ●
100% cotton fabric, wool batting, fiber-reactive
dye; dye painted, machine quilted ● Photo
by Brian Sprouse

INGE MARDAL and STEEN HOUGS ● FACING NORTH, 2008 ● 48^{13}/$_{16}$ x 64^5/$_8$ inches (124 x 164.1 cm) ●
100% cotton; hand painted, machine quilted ● Photo by artists

BARBARA E. FRIEDMAN ● TREASURE, 1997 ● 21^1/$_2$ x 43 inches (54.6 x 109.2 cm) ● Cotton,
crystalline tulle; machine soft-edge appliquéd, machine quilted ● Photo by Arnold L. Friedman

LENORE H. CRAWFORD ● BOY ON THE BEACH, 2007 ● 30 x 37 inches (76.2 x 94 cm) ● Fabric, fabric paints, thread, cotton batting ● Photo by artist

CHERYL DINEEN FERRIN

MOTORCYCLES AND QUILTS MAY SEEM LIKE an improbable combination, but Cheryl Dineen Ferrin's portraits of riders are filled with power and personality. The riders' strong faces, usually portrayed with their "shades" on, fill the frames of these art quilts. Their bikes are not necessarily in the picture, but you know immediately that they're nearby. Created in appliquéd, hand-dyed silks and cottons, these portraits exude self-confidence and attitude. Ferrin's recent portraits of Blackfeet Indian artists, created for the Friends of the Museum of the Plains Indian in Browning, Montana, similarly capture each sitter's personality and spirit.

BLACKFEET PORTRAIT PROJECT: JOHN PEPION, 2011 ● 48 x 54 inches (121.9 x 137.2 cm) ● Hand-dyed silk and cotton, commercial cotton ● Photo by artist

Dyeing Silks

You can't just walk into your corner fabric store and say, "Hi! I'd like seven different shades of African-American flesh tones, please." So, out of necessity, I hand dye the majority of the fabrics I use in my portraits. This is at once the most challenging and the most rewarding aspect of fiber work for me. Fabric dyeing is part science, part skill. Occasionally, it involves a lot of finger-crossing.

Since my portraits are characterized by broad, flat areas of color, I spend a significant amount of time making sure that I get the unblemished shades I seek. Dyeing silk to create 12 different flesh tones is definitely the most difficult thing I deal with in making a portrait. Attention to every detail is required in the dye process, along with copious notes to ensure I can recreate a specific color if the need arises. I prefer to create shading or gradients on the fabric through the use of a darker shade of the fabric itself or through a dyed tulle overlay. I don't add pigment to the fabric once the dye process is complete.

MOTORCYCLIST PORTRAIT PROJECT: KARI AND JIM, 2007 ● 64 x 72 inches (162.6 x 182.9 cm) ● Hand-dyed silk and cotton, commercial cotton, faux lamé ● Photo by artist

Finding Models

I love having the opportunity to create portraits of people I know. I get inspired by the sight of their spiky gray hair or their faces bathed in sunlight on a windy fall day. Other times, I'm struck by the power I see in someone who simply shifts her weight into a graceful stance, and I'm driven to capture that presence.

I create most of my works in series. My *Motorcyclist Portrait Project* includes some people who are close to me, but I barely know most of the riders. I used Internet discussion groups and a network of friends who ride to put out a call for motorcyclists to model. I've been known to take my business cards and postcards and approach groups of motorcyclists to see if any interesting-looking individuals will allow me to create their portraits. My objective is to portray a cross-section of those involved in the sport.

MOTORCYCLIST PORTRAIT PROJECT: KEVIN, 2009
● 96 x 42 inches (243.8 x 106.7 cm) ● Hand-dyed silk and cotton, commercial cotton, faux lamé ● Photo by artist

MOTORCYCLIST PORTRAIT PROJECT: BILL, 2010 ● 45 x 33 inches (114.3 x 83.8 cm) ● Hand-dyed silk and cotton, commercial cotton ● Photo by artist

The *Blackfeet Portrait Project* participants were selected by the Friends of the Museum of the Plains Indian, the group sponsoring my visiting-artist position in Browning, Montana. The Friends provided a list of artists, and we conducted interviews to confirm their levels of interest in participation. Our initial list of 15 artists was created as a result of these interviews.

Their Eyes

I place each of my subjects very close to the foreground, forcing a direct interaction with the viewer. Their eyes determine how much I reveal about them in their portrait: Will they confront the viewer or avert their eyes? Can I convey more about this person with a crisply defined eye, or do I shield their gaze from the viewer? When these questions are resolved, I distill the image of the eyes to the simplest shapes that retain the individuality of the subject.

Step-by-Step Process

1. Select the individual to be portrayed. Interview him or her and discuss pose options.

2. Schedule a reference photo shoot and take 30 to 100 images in a couple of different poses.

3. Review reference photos and select a pose.

4. Using pen and ink, draw the individual from the selected photos.

5. Scan the initial sketch into Photoshop. Clean up the sketch so that each color area becomes a self-contained shape. At this stage, I'm creating a large, hand-drawn, paint-by-numbers pattern.

6. Fill each shape on the sketch with the appropriate color for the fabric.

7. Submit the color sketch to the individual for approval. Make any revisions required.

8. Hand dye the fabrics for the portrait to match the approved sketch.

9. Enlarge the portrait pattern using Photoshop and print it out in its actual size.

MOTORCYCLIST PORTRAIT PROJECT: LAURA, 2012 ● 72 x 32 inches (182.9 x 81.3 cm) ● Hand-dyed silk and cotton, commercial cotton, faux lamé ● Photo by artist

Cheryl Dineen Ferrin

BLACKFEET PORTRAIT PROJECT: LEON RATTLER, 2012 ●
63 x 41 inches (160 x 104.1 cm) ● Hand-dyed silk and cotton,
commercial cotton ● Photo by artist

10. Trace each piece of the portrait onto paper-backed fusible web.

11. Fuse each piece to its appropriate color fabric.

12. Cut out the fused fabric pieces and reassemble the portrait—like a jigsaw puzzle.

13. Fuse the pieces to a foundation fabric.

14. Finish the edges of each color area with satin-stitch embroidery, or with a neutral tulle cover.

15. Quilt the portrait and finish the edges. Add a hanging-rod pocket and a foot pocket for a hanging weight if needed.

16. Label and photograph the work. Record information about the artwork in my inventory database.

Sketch Stage Is Critical

My completed and approved sketch is, with very few exceptions, exactly what the final portrait will look like. Before I dip fabric in dye, print the pattern, or cut fusible, I know my final objective. We work out virtually all the bugs in the sketch stage, so the potential for surprise in the construction stage is minimized. I know a piece is going well when I feel I'm looking at a realistic depiction of the individual in a balanced composition—and when the prospect of making modifications to the image gives me a sense of trepidation.

If a sketch isn't going well, I analyze the situation. I critique the composition, the rendition of the individual, and the background to isolate problem areas. Occasionally, I can re-sketch the problem section and insert it in the portrait. If things have really gone wrong, I'll step back from the portrait for a few days—or weeks. When I come back to it, I'll start over with another sketch or a new pose.

Perception of Truth

I find few subjects as fascinating as the individual. Personal identity is a central theme in my work. My quilted fabric portrayals draw on the complex interaction between subject and artist to capture the individual's spirit. In the creative process, I strive to integrate prevailing attitudes on beauty, politics, and self-image. I want to represent a perception of truth—the moment that will tell something about the subject, the viewer, and the artist.

BLACKFEET PORTRAIT PROJECT: DAWN CHRYSTINE DAVISON, 2011 ● 58 x 44 inches (147.3 x 111.8 cm) ●
Hand-dyed silk and cotton, commercial cotton, faux lamé ● Photo by artist

Cheryl Dineen Ferrin

YOSHIKO KURIHARA

A FANTASTIC PARTY ALWAYS SEEMS TO BE IN FULL SWING—you can almost hear the music in Yoshiko Kurihara's art. Intricate quilting fills the backgrounds with symbols that expand on the themes of the pieces. Careful use of commercial fabrics—especially fabrics with graduated colors—creates costumes and decorations for the scenes. Kurihara's tall, thin, angular characters express a wide range of emotions through their body language: some are fizzing with excitement and some are slumped with despondency, while others seem to be cheerily contemplating the start of a new day.

WINE BAR II, 2003 ● 81 x 66 inches (205.7 x 167.6 cm) ● Cotton, lamé; machine pieced and quilted, hand and machine appliquéd ● Photo by Tsuyoshi Kurihara

Comparisons with Painting

I majored in oil painting in school and worked as an illustrator and designer for several years after graduation. When I got married, I became a full-time homemaker. Then I started quilting, which—since it mainly uses fabric and thread—is a convenient means of self-expression for a housewife. I can work on the quilts at my own pace between housekeeping tasks. The work can also be done in a small space, such as the corner of my living room or in my kitchen. Although fabric and thread are familiar materials that can be obtained easily, I enjoy adding interesting effects through the use of other types of textiles, such as vinyl.

In fiber art, the necessary colors can't be produced by mixing different pigments together. Moreover, it's difficult to express shadow and line when using fiber, compared with painting brushstrokes or using a pen. So using fabric is accompanied by some inconvenience. But it's a very exciting challenge to complete the work as I envision it through careful fabric selection, the use of a color scheme, and the choices I make about cutting and quilting. It's fun to see an unexpectedly good result emerge that I hadn't originally intended.

CONGRATULATIONS AND THANK YOU!, 2010 ● 78 x 59 inches (198.1 x 149.9 cm) ● Cotton, lamé; machine pieced, quilted, and appliquéd ● Photo by Tsuyoshi Kurihara

A WINTER STORY—FORLORN, 2006 ● 83 x 81 inches (210.8 x 205.7 cm) ● Cotton, lamé; machine pieced, quilted, and appliquéd, hand embroidered ● Photo by Tsuyoshi Kurihara

Always Carry a Sketchbook

I always carry a camera and a small sketchbook when I travel, and I have a pen and a sketchbook placed near the television in the living room. Ideas can be found in all places and mediums—on a street corner or at an art museum, in a movie or a TV show. When I see something that captures my interest, I immediately draw a rough sketch of it, noting the coloration, the shape, and what I feel or what impresses me the most. I look at these sketches and memos from time to time. When I decide to make a piece, I create a final sketch. At this stage, I'll get a model to pose for me,

and I may take photographs as well so that I can confirm my concept of the figure.

Elongated Figures

My figures are tall and elongated as a result of trying to express the figure sharply and linearly. In the case of decorative works such as *A Winter Story* and *Masquerade*, I think that portraying the people in this way creates a fantastical, mystical feeling. In the works showing everyday scenes from today's society, such as *Wine Bar II* and *City-Summer*, I enhanced the

DREAM, 2010 ● 83 x 65 inches (210.8 x 165.1 cm) ● Cotton, lamé, beads; machine pieced and quilted, hand and machine appliquéd, hand embroidered ● Photo by Tsuyoshi Kurihara

fashionable and urbane atmosphere by portraying people with slim and angular body shapes. I think that this simplified form emphasizes the motion of the figures and expresses it in a way that's interesting.

Advantages of Batiks

I prefer to use multi-colored batik fabrics. I think that the choice of fabric in a quilt is comparable to the use of paints in painting. Threadwork is comparable to using colored pencils. I like to use unevenly colored batiks, multi-colored ones in particular, because when I cut them carefully to make use of the parts with color gradation or color spots, they add depth and shadows to my work. I also prefer to use shiny metallic fabrics such as lamé or satin when I'm working on a fantasy piece since those fabrics increase the impact of the work.

I use commercial fabrics and don't dye or paint them myself. If I wanted to use dyeing and painting to alter the fabrics, I'd be better off painting a picture instead of making a quilt.

MASQUERADE, 2005 ● 86 x 83 inches (218.4 x 210.8 cm) ● 100% cotton, lamé; machine pieced, quilted, and appliquéd, hand embroidered ● Photo by Tsuyoshi Kurihara

Process of Making "Masquerade"

Masquerade is a good example of my process. This quilt was inspired by the masquerade scene in the musical *The Phantom of the Opera*. I wanted to create a fantastical atmosphere that mixed reality and unreality. I decided that the figures would be designed decoratively and linearly. Instead of determining the overall composition in advance, I started the work by sketching various figures on graph paper. When I was satisfied with the results, I enlarged the sketch of the figures so that they were the actual size they'd be in the piece. I made each figure separately using piecing

over freezer-paper patterns. I put the five finished figures on the wall and rearranged them, moving them up and down until I found a satisfactory layout. Then I sewed everything to the stage.

Next I arranged the drop curtain across the upper part of the piece. I also decorated the piece with braid and tassels and appliquéd on the masks. Just like the story of Sleeping Beauty, when roses cover the castle and prevent an invasion from the external world, the hedge of black roses in my quilt separates the figures in the piece from the viewer. Through the use of gold

MORNING BREEZE, 2009 ● 90 x 62 inches (228.6 x 157.5 cm) ●
Cotton; machine pieced and quilted, hand and machine appliquéd, hand
embroidered ● Photo by Tsuyoshi Kurihara

and silver lamé and a monotone-colored fabric with some gradation, I added glamorous, fantastic touches and chic coloration.

I usually put my work-in-process on the wall, so I can view it from a distance. If I feel uncomfortable with some part of it, I'll change the color scheme, the size, or the layout and sew it again. I'll repeat this process until I get a result that I'm satisfied with. Sometimes I can't find a satisfactory solution, no matter how much I try. When this happens, I stop working on the quilt and put it aside. Six months to a year later, I'll bring it out again. Sometimes, unexpectedly, I'll be able to resolve the design problems that I had with it.

Invitation into My World

I'm not sure that my quilts reflect my lifestyle, but I do have many friends and often invite them over. I like to have my home full of people. I also like to go to restaurants, and I enjoy lively celebratory occasions, such as family birthdays and anniversaries. Whenever I make a quilt, I try to create a story that invites viewers into the world of its fairy tale.

● Yoshiko Kurihara

LORA ROCKE

LIKE TURNING THE PAGES IN AN OLD FAMILY PHOTO ALBUM, viewing Lora Rocke's work gives us glimpses into lives from another era. Even the pieces based on contemporary images have a nostalgic feel to them. They are like memories grown fuzzy with time. Careful fabric selection creates this feeling of age. Heavily layered threadwork captures the details of expression. A certain red punctuates much of Rocke's work: red lipstick, red high heels, red bowling uniforms, red borders, the red of her signature L chop. Yet this red is for reminiscence—regret, perhaps, for times gone by.

IN HER SISTERS' SHADOW, 2011 ● 36 x 24 inches
(91.4 x 61 cm) ● 100% cotton fabrics, untreated canvas,
cotton and cotton-blend thread; hand tinted, handwrit-
ten, machine pieced, appliquéd, stitched, and quilted ●
Photo by artist

Physical Connection with Fiber

I've always loved the feel of fabric, fibers, wovens, and threads. There's a definite physical connection between the surface of the work and me, but drawing is the foundation of all of my work. I make fluid drawings that help me create appliqué patterns. I also draw with my sewing machine. Since I can't mix colors for thread like you can with paint, I've created a technique of layering thread that gives the illusion of a certain color or tone. The direction in which the threads are stitched mimics the way lines are layered in a drawing, and the layers of thread give the portrait depth and volume. The physical movement of applying the stitches and the multiple layers of thread required for creating facial features are similar to brushstrokes in painting.

The most pleasurable aspects of creating a fiber-and-thread portrait are the sorting and the stitching. There's something almost Zen-like about looking through stacks of fabrics to find that perfect piece, about discovering the exact section that may create a shadow or an indication of a brow, about lining up

ONE LAST LOOK 1952, 2010 ● 20 x 16 inches (50.8 x 40.6 cm) ● 100% cotton, 100% wool, cotton and cotton-blend thread; machine pieced, appliquéd, stitched, and quilted ● Photo by Orville Jones

IN THE SUMMER OF '59, 2011 ● 23 x 35 inches (58.4 x 88.9 cm) ● 100% cotton fabrics, cotton and cotton-blend thread; hand tinted, machine pieced, appliquéd, stitched, and quilted ● Photo by Orville Jones

BOWLING TEAM TOAST, 2008 ● 17 x 28 inches (43.2 x 71.1 cm) ● 100% cotton fabrics, untreated canvas, cotton and cotton-blend thread; machine pieced, appliquéd, stitched, and quilted ● Photo by Orville Jones

threads from highlight colors to deep tones. The portraits that I create in fiber and thread are prompted by the pure, lovely feel of the fabrics—the thrill of creating depth and dimension through layers of thread and the physical movement of applying all the layers.

Yet, in the end, there's a certain amount of serendipity, of surprise at the results. There's a breathless uncertainty in the process. I have to listen to the work and be open to change. Total control can be the death of a piece.

Hatbox of Old Photographs

My main source of inspiration is old photographs, and my search for images is ongoing. I keep the bulk of my current photo collection in an old hatbox. I keep images of families and multiple generations. Most of the hatbox photos date from the late 1890s through the 1940s, but some are contemporary images taken during my lifetime. I collect photos from my albums and from family archives. I search through bins at antique shops and flea markets. I love contemporary life, but my portraits deal with memories—even recent memories. They're snapshots of life: short, sweet, fading.

When contemplating a new piece, I'll sometimes look through the hatbox with a purpose in mind. For example, I may search for women in hats, children with pets, sisters, etc. When selecting images for my stitched portraits, I look for a personal connection or a kindred feeling. One or two photos usually come to the fore and speak to me: "Here is my story," they say.

I Know Women Best

I feature images of women in my work because "I do what I know best." I know women. They're my friends and part of my family. I know the curve of a woman's cheek, the sturdiness of her stance, her emotions, friendships, and children. I find that I'm drawn to telling women's stories because I know their stories. I share their emotions. They're friends of mine, sisters from another time, women I'd like to know. Creating their portraits allows me to share my own feelings of friendship, loss, joy, longing, and hope.

FORWARD GLANCE, 2006 ● 36 x 18 inches (91.4 x 45.7 cm) ● 100% cotton fabrics, cotton and cotton-blend threads; machine pieced, appliquéd, stitched, and quilted ● Photo by artist

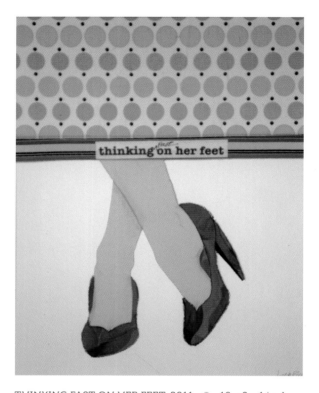

THINKING FAST ON HER FEET, 2011 ● 10 x 8 x 1 inches
(25.4 x 20.3 x 2.5 cm) ● 100% cotton, handmade paper,
pencil; machine quilted ● Photo by artist

COOLING HER HEELS, 2010 ● 10 x 8 x 1 inches
(25.4 x 20.3 x 2.5 cm) ● 100% cotton, handmade
paper, pencil; machine quilted ● Photo by artist

I Love Shoes!

Like many women, I love shoes! My fascination began
way back when, with my mom's size 4 feet. She had
the greatest collection of high-heeled shoes when I
was young. I loved clomping around in her shoes. I felt
so grown up and so pretty. I still feel that way when I
put on a great pair of shoes.

I often work in series. I try out techniques, ideas,
and subjects. I call them my "Smalls," as the pieces
are no larger than 14 x 11 inches (35.5 x 27.9 cm),
fabric sketches really. These pieces allow me to
play with an idea, with fabric combinations, stitching styles, or different media without investing too
much in time or material. *Shoes with Attitude* was
one of those series.

Tell a Story Visually

My process begins with the image. I search through
my hatbox collection, pulling out four or five photographs that speak to me. These images are enlarged
on my copier until they're big enough for me to see
their details. I then create contour drawings of my
subjects, editing and enhancing as I draw.

One of the drawings usually calls out, "Me first!" I
pin that enlarged drawing front and center on my
design wall and begin the process of getting to know
its characters. After all, I'm trying to tell their story
visually. They begin to be my friends. I get to know
if their eyes crinkle when they smile, if they're sober
or silly, what they may be thinking. I often imagine a
storyline to help me make some decisions. This may
take a few days or a few weeks. When I have all of my
thoughts together, I usually know just what fabric

will be used as the background and how the characters will be clothed. I search through my cupboards for the appropriate fabrics or make trips to my local quilt shops—on a mission.

Next, I sort through varying shades of fabrics, finding just the right ones to indicate a shadow, the curve of a cheek, or the hint of a brow. This selection process often helps me to discover just who this person is and how to portray her personality. I then create the appliqué pieces and assemble the work. The final step is the thread. By this time, it's pretty clear to me whether the figure/face will be intensely stitched (thread driven) or stitched with fluid contour lines enhancing the appliqué (fabric driven).

I Am a Storyteller

I hope that those who view my works remember them as a dialogue with the subject, that they not only discover the intensity of stitching in each piece but also recognize the people and times that I portray. I hope that they're drawn in to look at the portraits more closely and to imagine the people stitched there. I hope that they wonder: "Who was she? What was her story?"

I'm a storyteller. Images, words, and people thread their way into and through my life and my work. By using layers of thread and cloth, I strive to create images that invite the viewer to invent stories of their own.

SOFA SOPHIA, 2007 ● 18 x 24 inches (45.7 x 61 cm) ● 100% cotton fabrics, cotton and cotton-blend thread; machine pieced, appliquéd, stitched, and quilted ● Photo by artist

community

RUTH DE VOS ● READ ME A STORY, 2010 ● 58³/₄ x 56³/₄ x ¹/₄ inches (149.2 x 144.1 x 0.6 cm) ●
100% cotton, fiber-reactive dye, fabric paint; hand dyed, screen-printed, machine pieced, machine quilted
● Photo by artist

GWEN MAYER ● EURO WINTER, 2005 ● 36 x 42 inches (91.4 x 106.7 cm) ● Flannelette, used denim, neckties, knits, cotton, wool, embroidery thread, pens, hand-drawn elements from artist photos; dyed, machine appliquéd, hand stitched and embroidered ● Photo by Loris Bogue

LURA SCHWARZ SMITH ● DANCING PEACE, 2002 ● 60 x 68 inches (152.4 x 172.2 cm) ● Cotton fabrics, ink, paint, markers; machine pieced, hand appliquéd and quilted ● Collection of John and India Sorensen ● Photo by Kerby C. Smith

NANCY L. KING ● BACKYARD BOYS,
2010 ● 27 x 42 inches (68.6 x 106.7 cm)
● 100% cotton; raw-edge appliquéd,
machine stitched ● Photo by
Cassandra L. King

PATSY KITTREDGE ● CALIFORNIA DREAMING, 2010 ● 27$^{1}/_{2}$ x 60$^{1}/_{2}$ x $^{1}/_{4}$ inches (69.9 x 153.7 x 0.6 cm) ● 100% cotton,
Angelina fiber; raw-edge machine appliquéd, machine quilted ● Photo by Jennifer Kittredge

BENTE KULTORP ANDRESEN ● DASSEHRA, 2011 ● 50 x 67 inches (127 x 170.2 cm) ● 100% cotton; fused appliqué, machine quilted ● Photo by artist

INGE MARDAL and STEEN HOUGS ● THRESHERS, 2008 ● 48³/₈ x 65¹¹/₁₆ inches (122.9 x 166.8 cm) ● 100% cotton; hand painted, machine quilted ● Photo by artists

ALICE M. BEASLEY ● ENTRE NOUS, 2010 ● 26 x 89 inches (66 x 226.1 cm) ● Cotton, silk; raw-edge machine appliquéd, machine thread work and quilted ● Photo by Don Tuttle

JEAN R. HERMAN ● THE EPISCOPALIANS, 2010 ● 36 x 52 inches (91.4 x 132.1 cm) ● Cotton, silk netting, paint stick, velvet, gel medium; machine quilted, collaged ● Photo by Ken Sanvitte Photographic Services

DEBORAH K. SNIDER ● GRAPEVINE: STUD MUFFINS, 2011 ● 41$^{1}/_{2}$ x 41 x $^{1}/_{4}$ inches (105.4 x 104.1 x 0.6 cm)
● 100% cotton, fussy-cut images from numerous fabric sources, rickrack, ball fringe; raw-edge fabric collage, binding, free-motion quilted, hand-sewn finishing ● Photo by Harold D. Snider

MARGOT LOVINGER

"CELEBRATING THE BEAUTY OF THE HUMAN FORM" is a phrase that springs to mind when viewing Margot Lovinger's work. Her portraits of people and studies of hands lovingly celebrate each individual's beauty and character. There's a sense of stillness in her work: her subjects seem unusually serene and comfortable in their own skins. Lovinger uses layer upon layer of tulle to create an amazingly realistic sense of depth and contour. Each portrait honors its subject's distinctive allure and grace.

NIGHT, 2004　●　46 x 35 x 2 inches (116.8 x 88.9 x 5.1 cm)
●　Cotton, nylon netting, nylon tulle; hand stitched, embroidered　●　Photo by Randell McGlasson

My Father's Death

I graduated from art school in 1993 and abruptly stopped making art. Without the inspiring environment and fully equipped studios I'd had access to at school, I felt somewhat lost. I spent most of my time with my father, who was terminally ill and needed a lot of support. Eventually, he required full-time care as he progressed from HIV to full-blown AIDS, so I left my jobs and spent all of my time with him.

He died in 1994. I was devastated and slipped into a deep depression. For a long time, I made no art and did little besides go to my job and go home. I had visited the AIDS Memorial Quilt with him a couple of years earlier, and it moved us both deeply. After his death, friends and family encouraged me to make a panel for him, but for a long time I didn't feel up to it. I believed the panel I made for him needed to be a perfect expression of who he was and how I felt about him, and that idea was so daunting that I couldn't make anything at all.

DEMETER, 2011 ● 35 x 39 x 2 inches (88.9 x 99.1 x 5.1 cm) ● Cotton, silk, nylon lace, organza, netting, nylon tulle; hand stitched, sequined, embroidered, and quilted ● Photo by Randell McGlasson

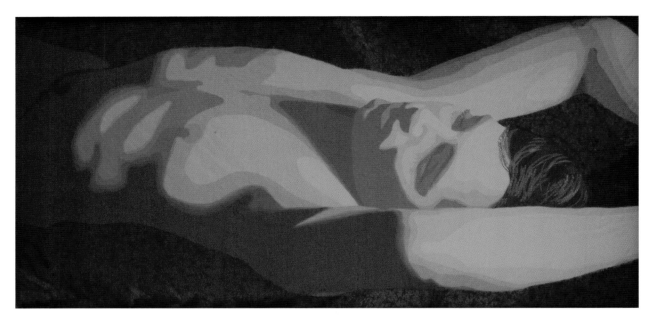

LIGHT SLEEPER, 2004 ● 23 x 48 x 2 inches (58.4 x 121.9 x 5.1 cm) ● Cotton, netting, nylon tulle; hand stitched and embroidered ● Photo by Randell McGlasson

VOLUPTAS, 2006 ● 29 x 58 x 2 inches (73.7 x 147.3 x 5.1 cm) ● Cotton, wool, silk, brocade, chiffon, organza, nylon beads, tulle; hand stitched, beaded, and embroidered ● Photo by Randell McGlasson

SURPRISE, 2006 ● 21 x 35 x 2 inches (53.3 x 88.9 x 5.1 cm) ● Satin brocade, cotton, nylon tulle; hand stitched and embroidered ● Photo by Randell McGlasson

Finally, I realized I could make a panel for him and send it in to join the quilt, and then make another panel that expressed something else and send that one in, too. I realized I could keep doing this until I felt I had said every last thing I needed to say about him. This realization freed me and allowed me to move forward and begin.

I made the first panel entirely out of his clothing in a crazy-quilt style and embroidered it with text that spoke of how much I admired and missed him. Making the panel for the AIDS Memorial Quilt got me

engaged in art-making again, and soon I was ready to make another piece. I continued working in fabrics and made a couple of very small quilts that were about my father's world and how it got smaller and smaller as he got sicker. I discovered that my real medium was fabric.

Hands Are Unique Expressions

I think hands are fascinating. I love looking at people's hands. They're so beautiful and expressive. From the calloused fingers of a guitar player to the delicate bones of a dancer, hands are unique. I make a lot of art about hands. It started when I saw how similar mine were to my father's. He and I did not look much alike, but when he lost weight during his illness, his hands—once large and mannish—started to look just like my own. It was wonderful for me to see that there was one way in which we were exactly alike. Suddenly, I loved my hands. I saw how strong and capable they were. And I loved everyone else's hands, too. I began making art depicting universal gestures that spoke to the interconnectedness of all people.

Why I Photograph Models

It's hard to say what I look for in a model. I'll meet someone whom I find fascinating to look at, and I won't be able to get his or her image out of my head. One of my models was a woman who happened to sit across the table from me at a huge dinner party and spent much of the night talking to the person seated to her right. She had such a striking profile that I couldn't stop looking at her, and by the time we were gathering our coats to go home, I'd asked her if she would model for me.

I photograph models rather than drawing them from life. I used to try to work from my drawings, but I discovered that while I could capture a lot of vitality and energy in a 10-minute drawing, I could really snuff the life out of it with a 30-minute session. However, the 10-minute drawing didn't allow me to capture enough detail to create a really realistic portrait. I now photograph my models and do drawings from the photographs.

Layers of Sheer Fabrics

I start by photographing a model and often take up to 200 pictures in a sitting. Sometimes I pick one photograph to work from, but more often I use elements from two or three different photos to get the exact look and pose I want. I do a drawing based on those photos and use that to map out the shadows and shapes that define the forms.

Next, I transfer my drawing to a transparency and use an overhead projector to trace the drawing onto a piece of lightweight canvas or starched cotton. The first few layers of fabric are usually cottons or silks, and I use them to rough out some of the major shapes of the piece. Then I layer sheer fabrics—often but not always tulle—over the base layers, cutting them away in some areas and stitching them down in others. Each successive sheer layer changes the hue of the layers underneath it in much the same way that a transparent color wash changes the colors beneath it in watercolor painting. This process of layering sheer fabrics and cutting parts away is what ultimately creates all the depth and definition in the image. Each layer is stitched in place by hand with tiny tacking stitches, so that nothing has a chance to shift around. In some parts, I'll use only four or five layers to achieve the desired color and depth; in other parts, I'll use as many as 16 successive layers of fabric.

When I'm done layering the sheers, I'll add some embroidery using thread or embroidery floss to help define some of the shapes or sharpen up the image, and then I may add beading or sequins. Some of the pieces are quilted, with the quilting stitches serving to outline and define the forms. Finally, the entire piece is stretched over a padded wooden frame.

My pieces tend to be fairly large. Usually the figures in my work are approximately life-sized or slightly larger. I've found that figurative art in which the figure is life-sized resonates more deeply with me than smaller work.

Beauty of the Human Form

My love of figurative art runs deep. To me, there's nothing more expressive, nothing more beautiful. People are fascinating and enigmatic in ways that nothing else can touch. I hope that when people observe my work they feel the sense of awe that I feel and know that they're not merely observers of beauty but truly a part of it. I want people to look at my art and know that they're beautiful and fascinating. They're divine exactly as they are.

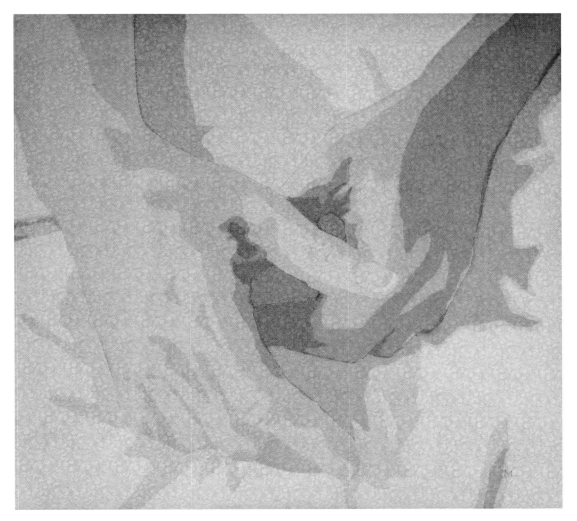

MORNING LIGHT, 2010 ● 23 x 25 x 2 inches (58.4 x 63.5 x 5.1 cm) ● Cotton, nylon tulle; hand stitched and quilted ● Photo by Randell McGlasson

ULVA UGERUP

WHEN ASKED WHAT VIEWERS SHOULD REMEMBER about her work, Ulva Ugerup replied, "Joy! Strength! Colors! Optimism! Great ladies!" Along with quirky hats, unusual embellishments, and a lot of embroidered text—some in English and some in Ugerup's native Swedish—that about sums up her work. Most of her texts exhort us to recognize the rights of all people to be treated fairly: to be able to practice the religion we want, to read what we want, and to wear what we want. Ugerup's work celebrates many famous women and their accomplishments, but, most of all, it shows the power of one woman to make a difference through her art.

SISTERS, 2008 ● 62 x 60 inches (157.5 x 152.4 cm) ●
Commercial and recycled cotton, paint, embellishments;
hand pieced and embroidered, machine quilted and
embroidered ● Photo by Agneta Bergström

Fiber Chose Me

I create in fiber because I like to work with my hands. I like to feel the material, to touch it, to put it together. I've always sewn—by hand for as long as I can remember, and by machine ever since I was big enough to carry my mother's Singer from the wardrobe and lift it up onto a table. She had an electric Singer from 1932. My mother was a modern girl, and that Singer is still going strong!

I can't say that I chose fiber; it chose me. I saw an appliqué work with a parrot in an exhibition when I was I child, and I clearly remember thinking, "I can do that as well!" That was the starting point.

There are practical advantages to creating in fiber: you don't need much space or equipment. It's rather clean. You can take your project with you—out into the garden, or on the train. And you're a member of a social network without comparison in any other kind of art.

Finding the Right Fabrics

For me, the most joyful task is finding the right fabrics. Nothing is chosen at random. Everything must mean something in connection with my chosen motif: colors, fabric quality, and the types of embellishment. Round forms and spirals are symbols of life, a heart or hands held over a heart mean love and importance.

THE NINE MUSES, 2006 ● 34 x 30 inches (86.4 x 76.2 cm) ● Recycled cotton, beads, buttons, vintage ornament; machine pieced, hand quilted and embroidered ● Photo by Agneta Bergström

COBRA, THE DAY MY SPECS BROKE OVER MY NOSE, 2007
● 12 x 8 inches (30.5 x 20.3 cm) ● Cotton, chiffon, Tyvek, sequins, wire, paint; machine pieced, hand quilted and embroidered ● Photo by Agneta Bergström

I try to find fabrics that work well together and "lift" each other. I recycle old fabrics that have a history, maybe a history that's just known to me and that brings back memories and feelings. My principle is that if you take the trouble to sew something, it must be there to be seen. Don't make small or anxious stitches—be big and bold! Thank you to Susan Shie for this good advice in her Lucky School of Quilting!

People and Politics

I have to like the people I portray. Otherwise, they don't qualify. They can be clever, courageous, talented, silly, dedicated, impossible, wanting to fight the police in the streets, shy, miserable, unhappy... I find photographs or painted portraits of the ladies, which is easy nowadays with the Internet. From these portraits, I make sketches—just pencil drawings, never in color—as free and personal as I can, so that they become "my" ladies.

I think art has a powerful influence. At times, it's regarded as a terrible threat. The Nazi idea of *Entartete Kunst*—forbidding artists to paint and burning books—shows us what a tremendous force art is. Sadly, artists and writers are still sometimes threatened with death sentences today.

I am a very small fish. I've always seen myself as an insecure person, but not when I'm creating. I may look like a rather insignificant, stout, white-haired, little old lady, but I know in my heart that I am wild and beautiful! Aren't we all?

I think it's up to you to decide how you want to live the only life that's been given to you. You have to make the best of it in spite of difficulties and sorrows. I'm an optimist and think things will end well. In my art, I'm free to express my joy, my hope, and my conviction that we will all manage.

"Ester Henning in Paradise"

I started with the quilt sandwich. Translated literally from Swedish, the name of the material I used as the background is "fellow-traveler fabric." In textile factories where they used to hand print fabrics, this material was run under the printed fabric to absorb the excess color. It was used over and over again. This type of fabric is almost impossible to get hold of these days. The piece I used was a gift from a friend. The frame is the backside of an old curtain.

ESTER HENNING IN PARADISE, 2010 ● 12 x 8 inches (30.5 x 20.3 cm) ● Commercial and recycled cotton, embellishments; machine pieced and quilted, hand embroidered ● Photo by Agneta Bergström

I made a drawing of Ester on paper from two photos—one with her fine hat and the other with her slightly lopsided smile and mischievous eyes. I put the drawing on top of the quilt sandwich and sewed along the lines on the machine, making very small stitches. Then I removed the paper. Because the stitches were so small, the paper practically fell off by itself. (This is a quick and easy way to transfer a drawing from paper to fabric.) Now I had Ester on the front and back of my quilt.

Next, we agreed, Ester and I, on the fabric for the dress: a Kaffe Fasset fabric with wild red roses. I put a rectangle of this fabric that was almost as big as the quilt on top of the quilt and pinned it at the edges. Then I turned the quilt upside down. I fastened the dress fabric from the backside along the seams from the drawing. Quick and easy! I then turned the quilt right side up and cut away the excess fabric from the dress.

BIRTHRIGHT OF WOMAN: TO READ WHAT I LIKE, 2005 ● 16^1/$_2$ x 16^1/$_2$ inches (41.9 x 41.9 cm) ●
Commercial cotton, wool, button, sequins; machine pieced, appliquéd, hand embroidered ● Photo by Agneta Bergström

ANGELS OF WRATH, 2008 ● 29 x 43 inches (73.7 x 109.2 cm) ● Mixed fabrics, vintage lace and necklaces, sequins, buttons, beads, shells, caps, found items; machine pieced and quilted, hand embroidered ● Photo by Agneta Bergström

Then I embroidered Ester's face in the same strong colors she used when painting portraits of the staff and the other patients at the mental hospital where she spent most of her life. But I didn't embroider her neck because I wanted her face to be sort of pushed forwards. I found the perfect buttons for her eyes. I made her hat from red velvet and yellow ribbon and decorated it with an old rusty beer cap I found in the street. We both liked that. I added yellow highlights to the dress, embroidered its edges, and hand quilted it. I used free-machine quilting for the rest. Then I embroidered the shoes, the hands, the wings, and the flowers, which were like the flowers Ester made. Finally, I added the text: "Ester Henning in Paradise!"

Halfway Through

I know a quilt is going well when I have a good feeling while working with it. But I know from experience that somewhere halfway through I'll find the work boring and wonder what the heck I'm doing! But I also know that it's important to get over this feeling and carry on. And when the quilt is finished, I can hang it up and sit down to look at it. And if it's good, it talks to me, and I'm happy. Then I have a cup of good strong Swedish coffee and just sit and look.

VIOLA BURLEY LEAK

STRONG GRAPHIC LINES AND SILHOUETTED FIGURES create unforgetable images in Viola Burley Leak's work. Filled with energy and power, these montages celebrate or decry important political and social events. Leak uses a variety of techniques, from appliqué and silk-screen to photo transfer and paint. Each part adds to the whole, creating compositions filled with intriguing detail and a range of emotion. While the meaning of some elements may be unclear without an explanation from a detailed artist statement, the overall visual force of Leak's work is compelling.

A CRY FOR PEACE, 2005 ● 57 x 56 inches (144.8 x 142.2 cm)
● Velvet, cotton, satin, metallic lamé, crepe; machine appliquéd and quilted ● Photo by Paul Richardo Elbow

Growing Up

From the age of four, I made doll clothes and designs out of fabrics that had been given to me by Mrs. Juanita Haynes, the neighborhood seamstress. She and my mother knew that I liked to work with material. I loved the colors, the feel, and the texture of the many different fabrics. I remember seeing my mother go out to dances in net evening dresses, and I thought that the fabric was so pretty.

When I grew up, I studied art at Fisk University in Nashville, Tennessee, with the renowned African American artist Aaron Douglas. I learned color and painting from Mr. Douglas. I used painting to simulate images and fabric, but the use of the actual fabric felt more comfortable to me. I left Tennessee and went to New York to continue studying in the department of fashion design at Pratt Institute in Brooklyn. Pratt was an eye-opening experience, because it incorporated fashion design and pattern-making with the study of surface design and textiles. I came to Pratt with a good background in sewing, because my next-door neighbor, Mrs. Ella Thompson, was a home economics teacher who worked hard to help me learn dress construction.

OBAMA QUILT: CHANGE, EXCHANGE, AND VISION, 2010 ● 54 x 45 inches (137.2 x 116.8 cm) ●
Cotton, silk, metallic lamé; machine appliquéd and quilted ● Machine quilted by Juanita Canfield
● Photo by Mary and Chas E. Martin

ME WE POEM: THE BAGS WE CARRY, 2008 ● 72 x 43 inches (182.9 x 109.2 cm) ●
Cotton, felt, velvet, sequins, organza, toy soldiers, silver spoons, handbags; silk-screened,
machine appliquéd and quilted ● Photo by Paul Richardo Elbow

Cut-Paper Silhouettes

My fiber work often resembles cut-paper silhouettes, because I also do collage designs. Fabric and paper in my mind are almost the same. I've used Japanese papers that tear less than fabric does, and there are papers that closely resemble fabric. I'll sometimes do a cut-paper design to plan the layout for a fabric quilt, because the paper produces good pattern pieces. The cut-paper technique also offers an opportunity to explore positive and negative space in a design. I use the cut-paper style to explore simple solutions to concepts. If the shape alone can tell a story, I don't need a lot of detail.

Tremendous Energy

My work is an extension of myself, and I have a lot of energy. I'm always working and thinking about the next step of action on a project. I try to solve a problem in many different ways before I make a decision. Sometimes ideas come immediately, and sometimes it's an effort. Because I can work in a variety of media, concepts from other art forms merge with the execution of the art quilts.

The energy I'm feeling about a topic can inspire and motivate the work. I can't imagine working without passion. My art reflects my outlook on life. I'm constantly being stimulated and reacting to my environment. My friends tell me that I seem to notice small details that they don't see. I think the details I see subconsciously reappear in my work. The energy around me is absorbed. There are so many possibilities, and it's a joy to discover new things.

Altered Fabrics

I alter fabrics when I feel that doing so is necessary in order to complement and complete the design. I use a variety of techniques: dyeing, shibori, painting, texturing with shredded fibers and netting, folding, and stitching. Before I started silk-screening, I used to draw with fabric paint and permanent markers. I started silk-screening images when I created an art quilt entitled *Jazz Montage 2*. It took me almost a year to make this quilt, because each panel used eight to ten color screens, and there were 16 panels.

Process of Creating "Addressing Hair"

The quilt entitled *Addressing Hair* was a lot of fun to do. I had just returned from the Spencer Museum in Lawrence, Kansas, where my quilt *Jazz Storm* was exhibited as part of the Aaron Douglas Modernist Exhibition. I'd been looking at and studying many of the book and magazine illustrations Douglas created, and I wanted to make a piece that was as simple, direct, and well-executed as his pieces.

Therefore, in this work, I decided to have many things come from one source: the black-and-white portrait of the woman would include all the elements used to style black hair. I included comb assortments, along with straightening-comb irons, curlers, brushes for hair coloring, assortments of hairstyles, and hair tracks for hair weaving.

The quilt began with a black-and-white sketch. After the sketch, I made a black-and-white ink painting. Then I made a drawing in black pen on white craft paper that was the same size as the quilt. Next, I made an outlined drawing on tracing paper to create

IN HONOR OF FAITH RINGGOLD, 2011 ● 36 x 36 inches (91.4 x 91.4 cm) ● Cotton, silk; printed, machine quilted, hand painted and appliquéd ● Machine quilted by Sue Moats ● Photo by Paul Richardo Elbow

ADDRESSING HAIR, 2008 ● 62 x 46 inches (157.4 x 116.8 cm) ● Cotton fabric and batting; machine appliquéd and quilted ● Machine quilted by Juanita Canfield ● Photo by Mary and Chas E. Martin

JAZZ STORM, 2006 ● 86 x 66 inches (218.4 x 167.6 cm) ● Silk, cotton; hand printed, silk-screened, machine appliquéd and quilted ● Photo by Paul Richardo Elbow

each pattern piece. I traced and cut out the pattern pieces one by one.

I put iron-on interfacing on the white background fabric to stabilize it and give it more body for easier handling. I applied a backing of fusible web to the black fabric that was to be cut out and attached to the white background. I then ironed on the cut pieces and attached them to the background. After all the pieces were ironed onto the work, I permanently attached

them with stitching and machine quilting. I even covered real human hair tracks in tulle and quilted them into the work.

With the completion of this quilt, I wrote a book entitled *Addressing Hair: Small Narratives*. The book contained short rhymes and illustrations about hair. One rhyme was: "Beauty is in variety of all kinds/a new hairdo can come with a change of mind."

JAZZ MONTAGE, 2006 ● 85 x 66 inches (215.9 x 167.6 cm) ● Silk, cotton, lurex;
machine appliquéd and quilted ● Photo by Paul Richardo Elbow

Fiery Social Issues

I like to do work about social issues. Sometimes these issues are fiery, because they involve a point of view and feelings, but feelings let you know you're alive and therefore give energy. I don't necessarily want viewers to believe as I do, but having a theme or an issue in my work gives me purpose. Selecting the thoughts and the visuals allows the picture to say a thousand words. The picture becomes the catalyst to evoke thought.

Making a good graphic is like working a puzzle that has many solutions. I enjoy trying to find the best answer. I do feel that art can change the way people see life, because it offers them another point of view. People can see and think what they want, but art can offer a variety of solutions and points of view. I believe that art, on conscious and subconscious levels, can influence and—depending on how open-minded a person is—change how the viewer thinks and feels about these issues.

icons

HOLLIS CHATELAIN ● HOPE FOR OUR WORLD, 2007 ● 81 x 81 inches (205.7 x 205.7 cm) ●
100% cotton fabric, polyester-wool batting, fiber-reactive dyes; hand dye painted, machine quilted
● Photo by Lynn Ruck Photography

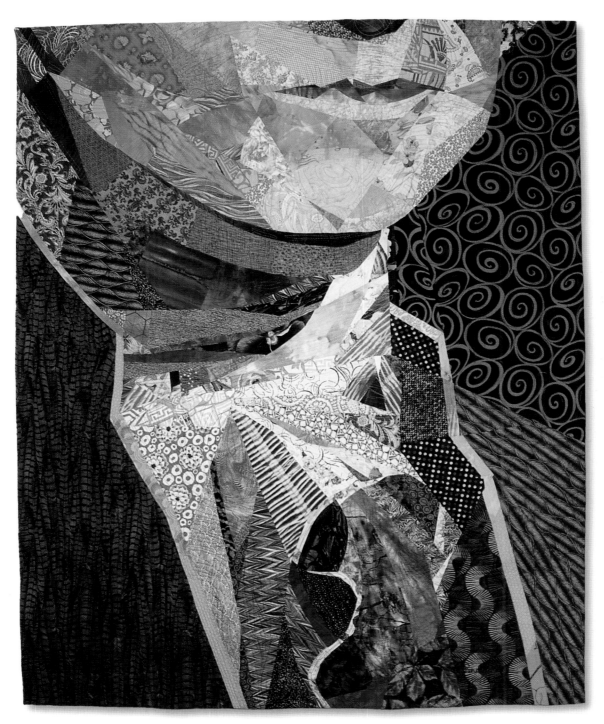

PAT PAULY ● GEORGE, 2010 ● 59 x 47 inches (149.9 x 119.4 cm) ● Cotton, polyester, commercial, and artist-made fabrics; machine pieced and quilted ● Photo by artist

MICHAEL A. CUMMINGS ● PRESIDENT BARACK OBAMA, 2010 ● 60 x 46 inches (152.4 x 116.8 cm)
100% cotton, textile paint; appliquéd, machine sewn ● Photo by D. James Dee

LAURIE CEESAY ● TINA, 2009
● 11 x 8¹/₂ inches (27.9 x 21.6 cm) ●
100% cotton, fabric markers, paintsticks;
machine pieced, raw-edge fused appliqué,
machine quilted ● Photo by artist

DIANA BRACY ● LOUIS "SATCHMO" ARMSTRONG,
2010 ● 40¹/₂ x 36¹/₂ inches (102.9 x 92.7 cm)
● 100% cotton, tricot, thread; fusible bond,
machine quilted ● Photo by Vincent Bracy

ELLIE KRENECK ● EXITING EDEN WITH ADAM AND EVE IN THE NEW RV, 2011 ●
45 x 34 inches (114.3 x 86.3 cm) ● 100% cotton, poly-cotton batting; hand painted
and appliquéd, machine pieced, hand and machine quilted ● Photo by artist

SHERRI CULVER ● WARHOL WARHOLLED, 2011 ● 24 x 23 inches (61 x 58.4 cm) ● 100% cotton, dupioni silk, brocade thread, metallic fabric; machine appliquéd and quilted ● Photo by artist

PAMELA ALLEN ● WANNA BITE? II, 2010
● 46 x 48 inches (116.8 x 121.9 cm) ●
Recycled and commercial fabric; hand
appliquéd, machine quilted ●
Photo by artist

MARILYN BELFORD ● THE WRATH OF POSEIDON,
2011 ● 53 x 59 inches (134.6 x 149.9 cm) ●
100% cotton; fused, machine-thread sketched,
long-arm quilted ● Photo by artist

DEBRA A. GABEL ● VENUS, 2003 ● 90 x 72 inches (228.6 x 182.9 cm) ● 100% cotton, fabric paint, metallic thread; machine quilted, pieced, raw-edge appliquéd ● Photo by artist

MARGENE GLORIA MAY

BOLD STRIPES, SPOTS, AND SQUIGGLES COALESCE in Margene May's art to create portraits that convey tremendous strength and warmth. An amazing array of hairstyles further expresses the personalities of the people she portrays. Working with fused appliqué allows May to make full use of a wide variety of ethnic and unusual fabrics, both cottons and upholstery blends. Many of her subjects stare directly at us from the canvas, yet their gazes are not confrontational but reflective. They share their feelings with us—feelings of love, pride, or regret. Our awareness of the variety of the fabrics' patterning disappears, so that we remember only the power of their emotions.

WATCHING U, 2010 ● 20 x 24 inches (50.8 x 61 cm)
● Mixed fabric; fused ● Photo by Thomas Stratton

Never Too Late

While I've always had an interest in creative pursuits, I didn't start making art until after retirement. The fact that I've gained a small audience for my work is a surprise to me and shows that it's never too late to pursue a new calling.

As an artist, I started with painting—acrylics, oils, watercolors, pastels—but my experiences always seemed to leave something to be desired. However, when I work with fabric, the pieces seem to speak and flow. I like the unlimited patterns and the results obtained by the juxtaposition of contrasting fabrics. Fiber also has a vibrancy and tactile dimension that I wasn't able to achieve with painting. My fiber art looks like a painting from a distance, but piecing various fabrics together creates a striking result unlike other mediums. Since I frame my completed fiber pieces under glass, they have a visual appeal similar to that of a painting but with the detailed piecing of a quilt.

SERENITY, 2009 ● 20 x 16 inches (50.8 x 40.6 cm) ● Cotton, cotton blends, yarn, canvas cloth; fused ●
Photo by Thomas Stratton

Margene Gloria May

JOHN, 2009 ● 22 x 28 inches (55.9 x 71.1 cm) ● Mixed fabric, cording; fused ● Photo by Thomas Stratton

A Bit of Attitude

When I tried my hand at painting, I was told I worked in a "painterly" fashion because of my use of bold colors and brushstrokes. I feel completely charged when I work, and this comes out in my portraits. The finished product is not always identical to my original intent. As I work, the portraits seem to tell me what to do next until I'm satisfied.

My work is both realistic and abstract, and it can easily be recognized by my use of bold colors, contrasting patterns, and a bit of attitude and whimsy. Features often extend beyond the perimeters of the frame. The endless choices available in fabric make this process both challenging and pleasurable.

Throw in Something Unexpected

I like bold, ethnic, and unusual colors and patterns. These palette combinations are drawn from my ancestral heritage. I primarily use cottons, but I also like the texture of upholstery fabrics. Although I use a lot of neutral colors to match the skin tones of my African American subjects, I usually try to throw in something totally unexpected, such as an African print design on the face, hair, or clothing. Leopard and zebra prints, black-and-white prints, and upholstery designs all find a place in my images. I often buy fabrics because of their visual appeal without a clue as to where they'll be used.

I use pastels or paints occasionally to add highlights, but I prefer to "paint" highlights and shadows with a

OPHELIA, 2010 ● 16 x 20 inches (40.6 x 50.8 cm) ● Cotton, cotton blends, canvas cloth; fused ● Photo by Thomas Stratton

contrasting fabric. I've experimented with dyes but find that the extensive resources of fabrics available from fabric stores, quilt shows, thrift stores, recycled clothing, and upholstery pattern books provide all that I need.

Eyes Are the Key

Attaining a realistic complexion and capturing the exact expression I want can be difficult at times. Usually it comes down to the eyes, which can show joy, sadness, defiance, or despair. These are some of the many emotions I try to capture with different images. Once I get the eyes the way I want, the rest is easy. A commissioned piece is more difficult, since the customer expects an exact likeness. It's a much

slower process, but I enjoy having the freedom to add my own insights into their personality.

I work with many variations of ethnic hair and use it to define my characters' personalities through color, texture, and style. By using fabric, I'm never certain where I'll end up until it's finished. Experimenting with how the hair can complement the subject's personality is also fun. This is one area where I really get to play with fabrics and let my imagination soar.

Light and Shadow

I focus upon everyday people who reflect or express an emotion. I'm attracted to the way light and shadow fall on a subject's face. I take photos, sketch, find

MEMORY KEEPERS, 2011 ● 20 x 16 inches
(50.8 x 40.6 cm) ● Cotton, upholstery blends, canvas
cloth; fused ● Photo by artist

U HAVE MY ATTENTION, 2010 ● 20 x 16 inches
(50.8 x 40.6 cm) ● Cotton, cotton blends, yarn,
canvas cloth; fused ● Photo by Thomas Stratton

reference images in magazines, and use those images as inspiration. A pose, lyrics from a song, or an unusual expression will stir up a memory that makes me want to add my own interpretation.

My portraits depict a moment in time, and my characters often speak their names to me upon completion. I also like to add titles that are a play on words. I named one piece *Goldilocks*, which is a reference to the classic fairy tale. However in the portrait, my character wears gold dreadlocks.

My Process

I sketch the portrait, and then I transfer the image onto canvas. I section off the face into shadows and highlights. In selecting the fabrics that will create the mood I want to convey, I use a variety of colors that may be warm or cool, complementary, opposites— anything goes. Once I'm satisfied with the design, I permanently fuse the pieces to the face and repeat the process with the clothing, the hair, and the background.

I like to review the picture as I complete each step to see if any color changes are needed before I go too far. If I'm dissatisfied with an area or if a selected piece of fabric doesn't work well, I simply fuse another piece in its place. The nice thing about this process is that colors or fabrics can be quickly replaced.

I know that a piece is going well when I step back and smile because I've captured what I wanted and am pleased with the end result. I often end with something very different from my beginning concept. If things aren't going well and I've changed the features or the materials several times, I'll put the piece aside and start on a different project. I work on more than one piece at a time, and there's usually another idea in the back of my mind for my next project.

Emotional Reactions

I want viewers who see my work to recall a memory of their own or to enjoy the expressions I've captured. My work is usually provocative and will evoke some thought—not necessarily one that's soft, pretty, or pleasant but definitely a strong emotional reaction. I work with contemporary subjects captured during a particular moment in time, and I try to express their feelings of sadness, regret and struggle.

GOLDILOCKS, 2009 ● 30 x 14 inches (76.2 x 35.6 cm) ● Cotton, cotton blends, yarn, canvas cloth; stitched, fused ● Photo by Thomas Stratton

LORI LUPE PELISH

IN LORI LUPE PELISH'S WORLD, PEOPLE CLEARLY have a lot on their minds. The figures in her vignettes seem pensive, worried. Even the mother in "Mother and Child" is lost in thought, "surrounded by good and bad intentions." Working with raw-edge appliqué and using a subdued palette of commercial prints, Pelish creates works that resonate. The worries of her characters reflect our own. Captured in the middle of an important discussion or absorbed in troubled contemplation, these figures invoke our concern. We want to know what's happening in their lives and we ache to offer comfort.

BOY DREAMS II, 2006 ● 38 x 41 inches (96.5 x 104.1 cm)
● Commercial cotton fabrics; machine appliquéd, quilted, and embroidered ● Photo by David Pelish

In Love with Fabrics

I came to the fiber medium on a whim. In college, I did an independent study for my BFA in silk-screen printmaking. One day I heard someone talking about a quilt, and I just decided to try to make a wall hanging. Although I encountered difficulties and challenges because I had no sewing experience, I was instantly in love with the huge variety of fabrics and with how fun it was patterning complicated shapes out of them. However, it wasn't until I moved from doing patchwork to creating raw-edge appliqué that I really felt a serious connection with the medium. I feel at ease with a pair of scissors in a way that I never quite achieved with pencil or brush.

Freeze-Frame Dramas

I've never been great at expressing myself verbally. I figured out early on that my work could do this for me. Each piece expresses my feelings regarding a topic that I'm concerned about. Over the years, I've made quilts depicting human reactions to war, inequality, family altercation and responsibility, living with violence, and the question of our place in the world.

FLIGHT OF THE HONEYBEES, 2010 ● 43 x 57 inches (109.2 x 144.8 cm) ● Miscellaneous fabrics; machine appliquéd, quilted, and embroidered ● Photo by David Pelish

HIDE AND SEEK: SANCTUARY, 2007 ● 32 x 91 inches (81.3 x 231.1 cm) ● Commercial cotton fabrics; machine appliquéd, quilted, and embroidered ● Photo by David Pelish

SAFE IN SUBURBIA, 2004 ● 41 x 69 inches (104.1 x 175.3 cm) ● Commercial cotton fabrics; machine appliquéd, quilted, and embroidered ● Photo by David Pelish

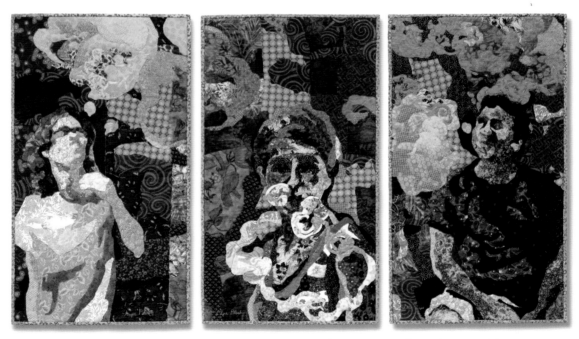

SOMETHING NOTHING EVERYTHING, 2011 ● 22 x 40 inches (55.9 x 101.6 cm) ● Commercial cotton fabrics; machine appliquéd, quilted and embroidered ● Photo by David Pelish

WE WERE ALL THERE, 2009 ● 43 x 130 inches (109.2 x 330.2 cm) ● Commercial cotton fabrics; machine appliquéd, quilted, and embroidered ● Photo by David Pelish

These are the subjects that capture my attention. I'm so affected by the harshness of what goes on daily. I want to fix, change, or reach goals that will make a difference. I tackle these subjects because of my own personal struggle to understand, learn, and improve. Sadness has a unique ability to attract and affect people, to make them stop, think, and feel.

Shifting Puzzle

In my mind, I create a shifting puzzle of figures, settings, and props. Once an idea starts becoming clear, I decide on whom to use as a model. I usually use family, friends, or myself, taking advantage of the familiarity and convenience. I borrow bits and pieces of their stories and intertwine them with my own impressions.

I use photographs. Like many people, I have a huge collection and constantly flip through them. They could be very old or purposely planned and shot. I'm always looking for expression, whether it's in a face or in an interesting pose that catches my eye. I also use figures that I've come across in the morning paper whose poses may trigger a response that coincides with my idea.

Beauty in the Not So Obvious

I remember as a child finding a flower growing at the side of the road. It was as small as the head of a pin, but it was perfect—beautiful and exquisite. I marveled that it was just a weed and felt it was unfair that hardly anyone would see it.

I've found that I enjoy looking for the beauty in the not so obvious. And I want to bring that interest to other people. I like the challenge of putting difficult or odd colors together and finding them transformed into clusters of exquisite beauty. The small patterned fabrics I use are a joy to work with; some are so finely detailed that they're works of art by themselves. I use the multiple colors in the tiny patterns to blend them together in order to achieve more complicated values and hues.

The Process of Making "We Were All There"

The initial inspiration for *We Were All There* started during a trip to Normandy, France. I encountered a vast, beautiful landscape filled with endless, precise rows of white crosses memorializing the soldiers of war and our hope for freedom. I was taken by surprise that a place so filled with tourists had this power to create an atmosphere of reflection and awe. It was quiet and dignified, and everyone could feel the importance of its history.

I wanted to create a large, panoramic piece that would capture the sense of cadence I got from my visit, a rhythm that would move you along with an ability to be read from either the right or left, to show the flow of time. I selected photographs of the people I planned on using and started working on quick sketches.

I always start with a piece of black fabric for my foundation. I pin it to my work wall, which is made of ceiling tiles and is porous enough for easy pinning. I use a white chalk pencil to draw a contour sketch of my figures and a line or two for the horizon. I purposely keep it simple; the details come later.

I start with a face. Capturing the precise emotion and character of the figure is important right from the start. Many times, the prints that I've chosen look wonderful in the piles of fabrics that I've sorted

MOTHER AND CHILD, 2002 ● 52 x 45 inches (132.1 x 114.3 cm) ●
Commercial cotton fabrics; machine appliquéd, quilted, and embroidered ●
Photo by David Pelish

on my floor but read poorly once placed in the face. It's necessary to stay relaxed and be prepared to change fabrics.

Next, I cut shapes with my scissors. I cut, place, and fit, rearrange, and build, stepping back occasionally to view the work. As I work, I decide on the details. For example, I liked the way the striped fabrics suggested a flow of time, a movement. I also decided to have a plant of some kind in each panel to represent the changing seasons and the passing years.

I do a free-motion meandering stitch with many different thread colors all over the piece to make my quilt top. I usually quilt an outline around each of the figures and objects and use more free-motion stitching in other areas to create texture and depth. When I

started working with rough-edge appliqué and introduced figures into my work, I needed to find a way to quilt them. My soft palette and curvilinear shapes wouldn't have looked right to me with a quilting line bisecting them. This led to my discovery of a method using zigzagged knots, similar in effect to a tied quilt. I use a rayon thread and many colors. These knots add texture and contribute more colors to the piece.

Beautiful Humanity

I'd love to think that people who have seen my work find themselves unable to forget it, that they made a personal connection to a particular piece. I'd like people to remember how expressive, thoughtful, and beautiful humanity can be.

ED, 2008 ● 33 x 26 inches (83.8 x 66 cm) ● Commercial cotton fabrics; machine appliquéd, quilted, and embroidered ● Photo by David Pelish

BOY DREAMS, 2004 ● 43 x 30 inches (109.2 x 76.2 cm) ● Commercial cotton fabrics; machine appliquéd, quilted, and embroidered ● Photo by David Pelish

SONIA BARDELLA

LOVE ENCIRCLES THE SUBJECTS of Sonia Bardella's portraits: lovers' arms twine around each other; a mother's arm protectively enfolds her child; a group of young women form a circle of friendship. Bardella uses a wide variety of rich hues and densely patterned fabrics to create colorful, lively settings. Her machine quilting adds interesting details, as the wind swirls across a seaside sky, or little girls play dress-up in an elaborate setting that seemingly exists only in their imaginations. Each piece creates an atmosphere of love and caring, of peace and infinite potential.

DO YOU REMEMBER?, 2011 ● 57 x 55 inches (144.8 x 139.7 cm) ● Cotton fabric, 100% silk, textile paints; hand pieced, machine embroidered and quilted ● Photo by Foto Piccolo

Filling an Empty Part of Myself

Even as a child I loved fabric, colored thread, yarn, and buttons. In clothing shops, I'd pass my fingers over the fabrics and imagine how to combine the colors and styles. I became acquainted with patchwork much later on, and the discovery was like filling an empty part of myself.

I've worked as an illustrator of botanical texts for university publications. I've also designed gardens. But patchwork changed my life. Creating through the use of different fabrics sewn side by side and taking advantage of the different patterns is much more interesting, imaginative, and difficult than painting. And the process gives me much more satisfaction. I enjoy giving attention to each small detail.

Unfortunately, I'm limited in how much hand-sewing I can do because of an accident that left me with an inability to move my right arm in certain ways. Even machine quilting can be a problem. I can work for about 20 to 30 minutes, then I must stop and do something else for a while.

FIRST DAY OF SUMMER, 2009 ● 62 x 43 inches (157.5 x 109.2 cm) ● Cotton fabrics, rayon threads, batik and nylon curtain, textile paint; machine quilted ● Photo by Foto Piccolo

THANK YOU FOR THE FLOWERS, 2007 ● 48 x 67 inches (121.9 x 170.2 cm) ● 100% cotton fiber, batiks, synthetic batting, cotton and rayon threads, textile paints; hand and machine quilted ● Photo by Foto Piccolo

Ideas for Portraits

I've always loved making portraits but had previously done them with pencils and charcoal. My first subjects were my children and, later on, relatives and friends. Now I might look through a magazine and see a photograph that I find interesting. I'll immediately think about whether the photo could become an idea for a new quilt. I may change the colors, the background, the position of the subjects, the clothing, etc. A photograph taken by a family member can become something entirely different when interpreted in cloth.

When I begin a new quilt, I start with an idea and try to imagine it in two ways: with a realistic setting, or with a stylized background. Then I pull out all the appropriate fabrics I have, put them on the floor, and try out various combinations until I decide which type of background to sew.

Initially, my most difficult problem was how to create faces, hands, and legs in fabric. Some of my quilting friends advised me to print my drawings on fabric using the computer, but I wanted to draw directly on the fabric and blend the colors. After searching for a long time, I finally found a type of oil-pastel stick that gives me the results I want.

ROLLING INTO SPRING, 2006 ● 35 x 64 inches (88.9 x 162.6 cm) ● Cotton fabrics, metallic and rayon threads, textile paint; machine embroidered and sewn, hand and machine quilted, appliquéd ● Photo by Foto Piccolo

Hair Is the Picture Frame of the Face

It's true that the hair on the figures in my portraits is very important. It helps me to define the personalities of the people I portray. Sometimes I paint in the hair as a frame around the face; sometimes I use a variety of fabrics, which are layered to give a shaded effect. I also use a variety of threads in at least four hues: dark, medium, light, and variegated.

"Thank You for the Flowers"

One day, while at the hairdresser's, I was intrigued by an old photograph I saw in a magazine of two young people kissing, seen from above. Although the photo was taken during wartime, all you could see was the couple's love. A few months later, I was moving into a new house and heard my dog bark. I went to the window and saw my son below in the garden kissing his girlfriend. I immediately thought of the photograph I'd seen in the magazine. I had to fix the moment in a quilt!

I took a photograph, from which I made a detailed drawing the size of a normal sheet of paper. I then enlarged it with a photocopy machine. On good-quality cotton fabric, I first drew the outlines of the faces and hands with a pencil, then went over the lines with a textile marker. I painted with oil pastel paintsticks to fill in the color and shading, starting with the darker colors and finishing with the lighter shades. I let this first layer dry for at least 24 hours, then evaluated the results. Where the piece seemed too dark, I added more light shading. To make the color adhere to the fabric, I used a sponge instead of a brush. When the portrait was finished, I added the last touches of light. I let the piece dry for 10 days, then ironed the fabric first from the back and then from the front using a dry iron set at a medium temperature. In the meantime, I pulled out other fabrics, put them side by side, and chose the ones I wanted.

Next, I created the clothes. I sewed them with Avalon water-soluble stabilizer and then removed it by dissolving it in water. Then I made the bench, which I changed from the original photograph. The fabric with the stones was a real find, but when I put it

Sonia Bardella

127

FIRST LOVE, 2010 ● 19 x 27 inches (48.3 x 68.6 cm) ● Cotton fabrics, silk and rayon threads, textile paint; hand and machine quilted ● Photo by Foto Piccolo

near the rest of the composition, something wasn't right: the shadows on the stones weren't the same as the shading on the figures. So, with a great deal of patience, I corrected the shading on each stone. To create the shadows on the bench and the ground, I used transparent curtain material: one layer for the wood, two for the crevices, and three beneath the bench.

For the hair, I used batiks. I ironed on fabric adhesive and cut the fabric into pieces to create the shadings I wanted. I then sewed the background to the bench, added the clothes, and—last of all—added the heads and the hands, which were cut with a seam allowance of ⅜ inch (1 cm) and appliquéd by hand. To create the frame of leaves and flowers, I used cotton fabrics that I'd dyed myself and several batik fabrics. The flowers and leaves weren't really there, but I created them by "drawing" freehand with the sewing machine, using laminated,

shiny, and variegated threads. I used a *broderie perse* technique to appliqué the girl's flowers. I did the quilting on the faces by hand and freehand machine quilted the rest.

The Beauty of Flowers

When I decide which fabrics to use for a quilt, I automatically decide what shape to give the quilt. Sometimes I start with an idea, which develops into something entirely different in the end, because there are elements I don't like as I go along. The process is intuitive.

I love beautiful things, and flowers are an especially important aspect of my work. My father had a garden nursery, and I studied natural science at university. I'd like the viewers of my work to go away with a feeling and a memory of having seen something beautiful.

PARTY DREAMS, 2010 ● 74 x 50 inches (188 x 127 cm) ● Cotton, silk, paintsticks, rayon and metallic threads; hand and machine quilted ● Photo by Foto Piccolo

family & friends

PHYLLIS A. CULLEN ● LOVEBIRDS (AND BABY MAKES) THREE, 2011 ● 16 x 20 inches (40.6 x 50.8 cm) ●
Commercial and hand-dyed cottons, paint; raw-edge collaged/appliquéd, machine quilted ● Photo by artist

SHARON TESSER ● THE DREAMCATCHER, 2011 ● 35 x 25 inches (88.9 x 66 cm) ● 100% recycled fabric, cotton, silk, paint; hand dyed and pieced, machine quilted ● Photo by artist

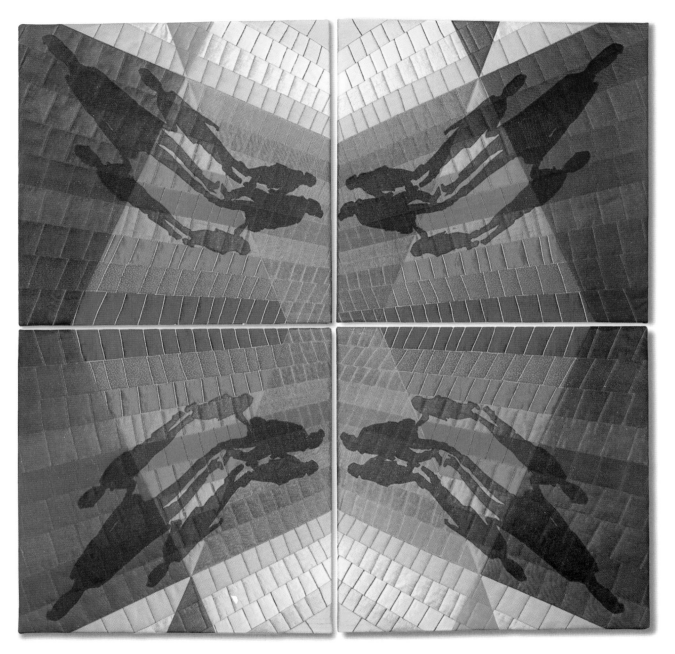

CYNTHIA D. FRIEDMAN ● THE OUTING, 2010 ● 32 x 32 inches (81.3 x 81.3 cm) ● Silk and silk organza overlays, cotton batting and backing, acrylic panel; machine pieced and quilted, hand drawn, cut, fused ● Photo by artist

LEA MCCOMAS ● TURKEMAN MOTHER AND CHILDREN, 2011 ● 39 x 45 inches (99.1 x 114.3 cm) ● 100% cotton commercial and hand-dyed fabric, cotton, rayon and polyester threads, tulle; raw-edge fused appliqué, thread painted, machine quilted ● Photo by Ken Sanville

TRISH JOHNSON ● DADDY READS TO IAN, 2006 ● 12 x 18 inches (30.5 x 45.7 cm) ● Cotton; machine quilted ● Photo by artist

OLGA NORRIS ● SERIOUS TALK, 2010 ● 24^1/$_2$ x 23^1/$_2$ inches (62.3 x 59.7 cm) ● Cottons, digital image; digitally printed, hand quilted ● Photo by Nigel Norris

SUSAN SHIE ● FRENCH TOAST: KING OF POTHOLDERS IN THE KITCHEN TAROT, 2011 ● 86 x 83 inches (218.4 x 210.8 cm)
● Cotton, Lunn fabrics, fabric paint, batting, thread; whole cloth, airbrushed, machine quilted ● Photo by artist

KATHLEEN KASTLES ● RAINY DAY PICNIC (SUV),
2011 ● 32¹/₂ x 31 inches (82.6 x 78.7 cm) ●
100% cotton, acrylic inks, aloe-vera gel medium,
thread; whole cloth, machine quilted ●
Photo by José Morales

MARGARET DUNSMORE ● FAMILY TIME, 2008 ● 38¹/₂ x 51¹/₂ inches (97.8 x 130.8 cm) ● 100% cotton,
buttons; embellished, machine pieced and quilted, hand appliquéd ● Photo by artist

GERI PATTERSON-KUTRAS ● COURAGE, 2008 ● 36 x 47¹/₂ inches (91.4 x 120.7 cm) ● Commercial cotton, acrylic paint, color markers; hand painted, machine quilted and appliquéd ● Quilted by Trudy Hardy ● Photo by Gregory Case

LENI WIENER

THE FEELING THAT WE MIGHT KNOW THE PEOPLE in her quilts is part of what makes Leni Wiener's work memorable. We sense that these are scenes we're familiar with. The figures in them are people we might have recently passed on the street. Wiener's work alternates between close-cropped intimate portrait studies, which focus on a single person's emotions, and city street scenes, where the backgrounds are just hinted at through a combination of threadwork and color patches. Masterful use of commercial prints and careful color placement create images that engage our imaginations.

THE EMPTY CHAIR, 2011 ● 19 x 19 x 1 inches
(48.3 x 48.3 x 2.5 cm) ● 100% cotton; raw-edge machine
appliquéd, machine thread sketched and quilted ●
Photo by D. James Dee

Fabric Is in My DNA

I work with fabric because I really love it. My grandmother made custom hats, and my mother was an interior designer, so maybe fabric is in my DNA. After years of working in a darkroom as a commercial photographer, I became sick from exposure to the chemicals used in film developing. So now I work in a medium that doesn't involve any chemicals or toxic fumes. Walking into a fabric store is exciting for me. I never alter the fabrics I use.

Fabric is part of my inspiration. I particularly love layering pattern on pattern and the complexity this brings to even a simple image. Finding just the right fabric is fun. Using an unexpected pattern makes a piece more interesting and intriguing than using a solid color. In the past, I used solid fabrics, batiks, and hand-dyed fabrics, but in recent years I've found myself gravitating toward prints and patterns in order to embrace and celebrate fabric.

PRIVATE WORLD, 2007 ● 54¹/₂ x 43 inches (138.5 x 109.2 cm) ● 100% cotton; raw-edge machine appliquéd, machine thread sketched and quilted ● Photo by D. James Dee

CROSSWALK, 2011 ● 18 x 23 x 1 inches (45.7 x 58.4 x 2.5 cm) ● 100% cotton; raw-edge machine appliquéd, machine thread sketched and quilted, mounted, stretched ● Photo by D. James Dee

Images with Quiet Power

Whether it's the expression on a face, the position of someone's hands, or a person's body language, I look for images that have quiet power. Body language is so expressive and so identifiable; I can tell a whole story just by the way a person stands at a crosswalk waiting for the light to change.

I work entirely from photographs. Because I was a commercial photographer, I see the world through a camera lens. Walking around with my camera allows me to capture images that speak to me in some way. I don't set out to take photos of something; I wait for the photos to come to me. The ordinary, the introspective, and the unremarkable snippets of the lives of strangers fascinate me—those internal and private moments that are so universal we don't even notice them but that we identify with when we see them. It's in these

quiet and pensive moments that humans are the most vulnerable and honest about who they are.

I consider my work to be a form of storytelling, but instead of telling viewers the story in my head, I try to create images that allow them to tell their own stories, to fill in the details from their own life experiences, and therefore to become more involved in the work. Nothing pleases me more than seeing people in front of one of my pieces discussing what the artwork is saying. This means they're connecting to something I've done.

Threadwork Backgrounds

I used to portray people in architectural settings, employing the perspective, particularly stairs, as a vehicle to draw the eye and create dimension. I enjoyed the depiction of the people in the images but grew bored with the creation of their environments. I decided to focus more on the figures and started to work toward eliminating, or at least minimizing, the backgrounds.

Sketching the backgrounds in thread with bits of fabric here and there to make them more dynamic allows for the creation of an environment without the need to be so detailed and specific. These sketches are done on white to lighten the background, making the figures more prominent—like watercolor washes on pen-and-ink drawings. After all, it's the figures I want to present to the viewer. Where the figures are is secondary.

Fabric Selection Is about Value

All my work begins with a photo or a combination of photos. I often manipulate the images in Photoshop until I like the final result. I use the cutout filter in Photoshop, applying it to one small section of an image at a time to assist in the simplification of value changes so that they're more easily translated into pieces of fabric.

Using my computer, I blow up each image in sections to the finished size of the artwork. I tape the sections together to form my working pattern. This allows me to trace every element in the image onto freezer paper so that I can cut the pieces out of fabric. I label every piece on the pattern with a number that corresponds to the value differences in that element.

Fabric selection is more about value than anything else. If the values are wrong, the image won't be successful. Color is important in setting a mood, and I use the concept of complementary colors to highlight or draw attention to where I want the viewer to focus. Working on one small element at a time, I build the

THE MAN IN THE BLACK TRACK SUIT, 2011 ● 22 x 26 x 1 inches (55.9 x 66 x 2.5 cm) ● 100% cotton; raw-edge machine appliquéd, machine thread sketched and quilted ● Photo by D. James Dee

Leni Wiener

141

OLD MAN, 2011 ● 29 x 25 inches (73.7 x 63.5 cm) ●
100% cotton; raw-edge machine appliquéd, machine
quilted ● Photo by D. James Dee

figures first and pin them to my design wall. This allows me to create a background that works with, but doesn't fight, the figures in the foreground. It's not uncommon for me to change a single small piece of fabric multiple times if I don't feel the whole image is working. A Ruby Beholder is an invaluable tool for the fabric selection process. Looking through a pair of binoculars held backwards also helps during the process.

When I like the way everything looks, I use little dabs of glue on a toothpick to secure each fabric piece, and then I sew the pieces in place onto batting. Sometimes I do the thread sketching or painting before adding the batting (if I want the stitches to sit on the surface of the fabric), and sometimes I add it with the batting (if I want the stitches to sink into the fabric). I only add the backing fabric when everything else is complete, and I use a minimal amount of quilting so the finished piece is clean and neat on the back.

When a piece is going well, I can't wait to get into the studio and work on it. I lie awake in bed thinking about every little detail and am anxious to continue. But if I find myself avoiding the studio and finding other things to do with my time, I know there's a problem and that I need to force myself to deal with it and get past it. I work on only one piece at a time and don't like to abandon anything in progress. I prefer to figure out what the problem is and deal with it so I can move on to the next piece.

I Want Viewers to Be Engaged

More than anything, I want viewers to connect with my work in some way. One of the most touching experiences I've had was at an opening of an exhibit when a woman approached me with tears in her eyes to tell me that one of my pieces reminded her of her recently deceased husband. And I once overheard a group of people discussing one of my pieces, a depiction of a young boy sitting on some steps outside a building. The people were arguing about what the boy was doing: Was he looking at something? Was he thinking, or maybe waiting for someone? Was he sad? Those people were engaged and involved with my work. I can't ask for more than that.

BITTERSWEET, 2011 ● 30 x 27 inches (76.2 x 68.6 cm) ●
100% cotton fabric; raw-edge machine appliquéd, machine
quilted ● Photo by artist

RUSH, 2012 ● Each piece: 15 x 15 inches (38.1 x 38.1 cm) ● Commercial cotton fabric; raw-edge machine appliquéd ●
Photo by Margaret Fox

MARY PAL

SOME SEEM WISTFUL AND SOME ARE FULL OF JOY, yet each of Mary Pal's portraits brims with life. The effect is similar to cross-hatching, but it is created using cheesecloth to produce portraits of amazing depth and emotion. Increasing the strength of color by increasing the layers of cheesecloth, she highlights the bright contours of her subjects' faces. We fill in the remaining spaces through our imagination. The unraveling edges on some of her portraits form the perfect metaphor for the physical and mental unraveling that can occur at the end of a life. Preferring to portray people who are often overlooked and ignored—the elderly and the homeless—Pal has created a portrait gallery of faces that exudes personality and wisdom.

MUSING, 2011 ● 24 x 20 inches (61 x 50.8 cm) ●
Stabilizer, cheesecloth, tweed coating, PVA glue,
monofilament thread; sculpted, machine stitched
● Photo by Ray Pilon

Time Versus Texture

With the sweep of a brush, paint makes a direct, quick statement. The same shape in textiles must be carefully cut from fabric, attached with stitching, and then layered with other fabrics. A shape on a painting may be spontaneously changed by painting over it; the changes on an art quilt are much more time-consuming to complete.

But the texture of fabric appeals to me. I'm drawn to the roughness of burlap, the drape of linen, the soft threads of cheesecloth. Stitching enhances this marriage of fibers and helps to unite these textural elements. Applying paint to canvas allows me to create a piece with a pleasing composition, but the same piece worked in fabric comes alive with a rich texture that moves the work into the third dimension with an irresistible tactile quality. Painted canvases speak to us through our eyes and our imaginations; art quilts do all that and then reach out to us with their familiarity because they're created from the same fabrics we clothe ourselves in every day. We are drawn to touch them.

HOMELESS LOVE, 2011 ● 34 x 24 inches (86.4 x 61 cm) ● Buckram, cheesecloth, burlap, PVA glue, monofilament thread; sculpted, machine stitched ● Photo by Ray Pilon

SOLACE, 2010 ● 44 x 33¹/₂ inches (111.8 x 85.1 cm)
● Denim, cheesecloth, burlap, PVA glue, monofilament thread; sculpted, machine stitched ● Photo by Ray Pilon

STOGIE, 2011 ● 32 x 24 inches (81.3 x 61 cm) ●
Buckram, cheesecloth, burlap, PVA glue, monofilament thread; sculpted, machine stitched ● Photo by Ray Pilon

New Technique

While working on a couple of abstract textural pieces, I combined a variety of shapes made of velvet, silk, and dyed cheesecloth, which I stitched down while pulling loose some of the fibers to give movement to the piece. My son, Mike, commented that he liked one of the pieces, but that I was holding it sideways. He pointed out that I had inadvertently created a shape in the cheesecloth that looked like the figure of an old man with his hands in his pockets standing with his back to the viewer. I was at first astonished and then intrigued: how could I accomplish this intentionally?

I decided to try wetting the cheesecloth with glue in order to sculpt it into position. And it worked. My first piece depicted an elderly woman sitting by a window. It was a very loose portrayal, with white cheesecloth where the light hit the figure and black cheesecloth in the shadows. I made a second piece, a study of the woman's face, using just white cheesecloth on a dark background and adding much more detail. As the pieces have progressed, I've experimented with dyed cheesecloth, details quilted in the background, and the addition of other imagery to accompany the figures. I feel that I've just scratched the surface of what I can say using this technique.

Backgrounds Create Contrast

One of the challenges with this technique is that there must be sufficient contrast between the cheesecloth and the background so that the facial features are recognizable. Black-and-white is the most obvious choice, but sometimes I want to add some warmth.

MEMORIES OF GOMBE, 2011 ● 34 x 49 inches (86.4 x 124.5 cm) ● Buckram, cheesecloth, scrim, acrylic paint, PVA glue, monofilament and cotton threads; sculpted, machine stitched ● Photo by Ray Pilon

I've started experimenting with sepia tones. One must be careful with the human face—getting too carried away with wild colors doesn't always have the desired effect. I remember playing with yellow cheesecloth on a purple background, hoping to achieve the effect of lamplight but ending up with such a ghoulish face that it had to be scrapped after an entire day of sculpting.

Cheesecloth-Portrait Process

The first step is the selection of a photograph. I take photos of someone I know or ask photographer friends if I can use their pictures. I've found portraits on the Internet and emailed the photographers for permission to use them. I've made wonderful friends this way.

Next, I think about the mood that I want to convey and decide on the colors that will contribute to that mood. I study the photo to make decisions on whether and where to crop it, and I adjust the brightness and contrast using Photoshop. Then I desaturate the image to reduce the photo to its most basic elements of light and dark.

Once I decide on how large I want the finished piece to be, I print out the photo using Photoshop's poster-printing option and tape the sections together. I place this under a sheet of Mylar and use a marker to trace the areas where the light strikes the face. I tape another sheet of Mylar over this, and I'm ready to begin. I take pieces of cheesecloth and brush them with a mixture of white glue thinned with water. I place these on the Mylar and adjust them using

SIZING UP, 2012　●　12 x 12 inches (30.5 x 30.5 cm)　●　Cheesecloth, buckram, acrylic paint; sculpted, machine stitched　●
Photo by Ray Pilon

a combination of my fingers, a paintbrush, and a wooden skewer until the wet fibers are densest in the brightest areas and more spread out in the shadows. When the face is complete, I let the cheesecloth dry overnight.

When the sections are dry, I peel them off the Mylar and stitch them down using monofilament thread, occasionally referring to my tracing for proper placement. Finally, I quilt through the layers, adding dimension to the features.

Going with the Flow

When things are going well, it's pretty easy to go from stage to stage without any hesitation or indecision. I try not to have a preconceived vision that the piece must live up to in the fabrication stage—there are always little surprises along the way, and they don't deter me. Very frequently the piece seems to have a mind of its own, and I've learned that there's more to be gained from going with the flow than trying to force things to go my way.

But working with glue can create "sticky" situations that can be very frustrating. I have painstakingly adjusted a small piece of wet cheesecloth until I got it just right, and then when I lifted my hand, the large section below lifted away with it. Sometimes the force is with you and sometimes it isn't, so in those latter moments, I take a break and make a soothing cup of tea. When I'm feeling fresher, I'll go back to my piece.

The Ordinary Is Extraordinary

My work attracts attention because it depicts ordinary faces in an extraordinary way. I believe each one of us has a story to tell and that our story is etched on our faces. The lines and marks that develop over time shouldn't be regarded as signs of old age but as badges of wisdom and experience. I like to think that when studying my portraits, viewers will reflect on what the personal history of the person might be. My portraiture frequently depicts the faces of people who are often overlooked or ignored: the homeless and the elderly. When viewers pause to examine the layers of cheesecloth in my portraits and take the time to study the lines that are there, perhaps this will serve as a reminder that time touches us all and doesn't diminish our humanity but focuses it. I hope that they'll take this experience with them and be more receptive to the face of the next stranger they meet.

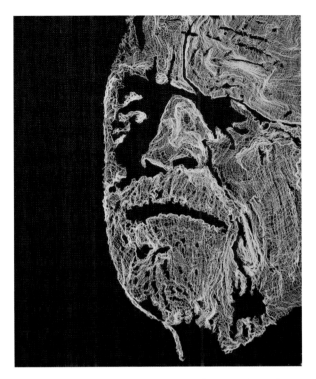

WATCHING, 2010 ● 20 x 16 inches (50.8 x 40.6 cm) ●
Linen blend, cheesecloth, burlap, PVA glue, monofilament thread; sculpted, machine stitched ● Photo by Ray Pilon

WAITING, 2008 ● 28 x 22 inches (71.1 x 55.9 cm) ●
Linen, cheesecloth, paint, PVA glue, monofilament thread; sculpted, machine stitched ● Photo by Ray Pilon

JENNY BOWKER

THE SATISFACTION OF A GOOD, HONEST DAY'S WORK radiates from the faces of the Egyptian men in Jenny Bowker's portraits. Her subjects are employed in a variety of occupations: safety officer, tour guide, glassblower, shopkeeper, craftsman. Featured with samples or symbols of their vocations, they are justifiably proud of what they do. Bowker's compositions are based on thousands of photos she takes herself and often combine simplified, pieced backgrounds with photo-realistic portraiture. Her images capture a sense of the men's quiet strength and personal warmth.

ABU ALI AND THE GILDED CHAIRS, 2009 ● 79 x 87 inches (200.7 x 221 cm) ● Cotton, synthetic fabrics, foiled jersey, hand-dyed fabrics; machine appliquéd, pieced, and quilted ● Photo by David Paterson

Rewards of Fabric

I went back to university as a mature student and finished my visual arts degree when I was 50. I majored in painting, but when I graduated I was painted out. I made a quilt just for fun. It was such a joyous experience that I made another and another. Then I realized that quilting was a medium and that anything that I could do with paint could be done with fabric.

Fabric engages people differently—and more. Most viewers will reach out to touch and stroke a quilt unless they're deterred. Fabric absorbs and enriches color and light, whereas paint often reflects and shines. Working with fabric also feels like a woman's language, which resonates for me because some of my early work was about women's issues. Plus, fabric has the benefit of portability. I can load an entire exhibition into suitcases and carry it around the world.

HASSAN AND THE GLASS, 2009 ● 79 x 60 inches (200.7 x 152.4 cm) ● 100% cotton, hand-dyed fabrics; machine appliquéd, pieced, and quilted ● Photo by David Paterson

HASHIM, 2007 ● 71 x 58 inches (180.3 x 147.3 cm) ● 100% cotton; hand-dyed and painted fabrics, machine appliquéd, pieced, and quilted ● Photo by David Paterson

Travel in the Middle East

I've spent 15 of the last 30 years living in the Middle East, following my husband as he pursued his career as a diplomat for the Australian Department of Foreign Affairs and Trade. I love the region. The people are warm and generous, the culture and history are interesting, and the food is wonderful.

People in these countries give friendship in a way that's rare in the West. We hold something back; they pull you into their circles and wrap you in a very whole-hearted affection. I wanted to make images of

men I like and admire, so that people could "meet" them. I wanted viewers to look into their eyes and to see that they were good men—straight and honest and hardworking.

Importance of Their Work

I decided that the work the men did should be a part of their portraits. Hashim, who seems to sit in the middle of a golden space, is a safety officer at Sakkara, the site of the first pyramid built in Egypt.

In fact, he's sitting at his base in a funerary corridor. I considered the idea of placing him against the image of the Stepped Pyramid but did not want the pyramid to detract from his portrait. A pyramid image in Egypt risks looking kitsch.

Ittayer runs a junk stall in the City of the Dead at the Friday Markets, and the clutter of objects around him almost seems to make him into one of the objects. I liked the idea of floating him among his wares. Hassan is a glassblower. The photo of him working with glass was strong and interesting, so it's the only portrait where the viewer can't look directly into the subject's eyes.

Thousands of Photos

I take thousands of photos. I like the way a photograph freezes a moment in time, so you can catch expressions and movements that wouldn't be possible with a sketch. I often take a string of 10 images of the same thing and find hidden treasures in the backgrounds.

When I'm in the Muslim world, I'm really careful about checking that people don't object to photographs. I'm also a bit devious in areas where I go frequently. I take pictures one week and return the following week with the prints—often a two-inch pile of photographs—to hand out. I love the process, as there's such delight in people's faces when they see their pictures. Egyptians don't often have photographs taken of themselves, except when they marry, and many of my subjects wouldn't have seen themselves since that time. Many of the people I photograph are old, because I'm really attracted to the way time writes history on a face. I'm often told that my photos are the first in 40 or 50 years that my subjects have been given.

Contrary to the popular belief that Muslims don't approve of images of people, there's been little objection in the countries where I've worked because my pieces are used in a secular context. With images of women, it's entirely different. While most women don't mind being photographed after I've gotten to know them a little, most of them would be deeply ashamed to have their images put on a wall in a Western art gallery. That's why all of my portraits depict men.

ITTAYER AND THE FRIDAY MARKET IN THE CITY OF THE DEAD, 2009 ● 79 x 58 inches (200.7 x 147.3 cm) ● Cotton, synthetic fabrics, polyester fleece, foiled jersey, hand-dyed fabrics; machine appliquéd, pieced, and quilted ● Photo by David Paterson

SANDSTORM OVER THE WHITE DESERT, 2010 ● 81^1/$_2$ x 97 inches (207 x 246.4 cm) ● 100% cotton, hand-dyed and painted fabrics; machine appliquéd, pieced, and quilted ● Photo by David Paterson

Geometric Backgrounds

I've always liked the combination of pieced patchwork with imagery. I think that pieced patchwork is an early form of abstraction. I'm also aware that the audience looking at my work is often made up of quilters, so my reference to traditional work is a salute to the work of women quilters of the past.

The pieced sky in *Sandstorm over the White Desert*, with my friend Magdy Badrmany, is appropriate in another way. Magdy is Bedouin, and Bedouins use diamonds or squares on point as common design elements around tents, in embroidery, and even as painted finishes around mudbrick doors in the towns where most of them now live.

Working Process

I think about the work for a long time before I start to reach for fabric. I usually play with ideas and jot things down in notebooks. I have a notebook that's a studio journal, and another one that's little and lives in my handbag. There comes a point where excitement about the work builds up enough to make me actually start.

I draw the men from the photographs. In many of the portraits, I actually trace the images from the photographs to be sure I have a true likeness. Using fusible webbing, I iron the portraits piece by piece onto a background of cotton on which I've drawn the composition. The portraits then hang on my design wall for a few weeks while I look at them. Because I know the men well, I need to be able to actually recognize them from the images, and that often requires a bit of fiddling and trying to work out why a face isn't quite right.

I stitch each piece down in invisible thread in order to anchor it. Some pieces are so small that they would fall off if they weren't stitched. When the top is complete, I quilt it heavily. The quilting is contouring, and I depend on it to give the men personality. I can deepen lines around eyes, create wrinkles, and shape noses and chins.

My Friends

I want people to look at my work and realize that they know and like my friends. I want the work to hover in their memories and surface when they're at rest or happy. I don't mind if they don't remember my name. I want my work to remind them that the Middle East is not about hate any more than any other area of the world is. It's just been given a bad name by a few extremists.

MOHAMED SA'AD, CARETAKER OF THE MOSQUE, 2009 ● 59 x 66 x $^1/_2$ inches (149.9 x 167.6 x 1.3 cm) ● Cotton, synthetic appliqué, hand-dyed and painted fabrics, threads; burned, machine appliquéd, pieced, and quilted ● Photo by Daniel Heather

work

JAYNE BENTLEY GASKINS ● OPTIONS, 2011 ● 33 x 27 inches (83.8 x 68.6 cm) ● Cotton broadcloth, inkjet inks, polyester and cotton threads; digitally manipulated photograph printed on cloth, thread painted, trapunto quilted ● Photo by artist

GALE WHITNEY ● FIRST SHIFT, 1999 ● 13 x 29 inches (33 x 73.7 cm) ● Cotton, wool, suede-like fabric, colored markers; hand appliquéd, hand and machine quilted ● Photo by Mark Frey

LOUISE SCHIELE ● TIME TRAVELER, 2011 ● 20 x 30 inches (50.8 x 76.2 cm) ● 100% silk noil, paint, 100% cotton, colored pencils, tissue lamé, 100% cotton thread; marbleized printing, machine appliquéd and quilted ● Photo by artist

TERI MCHALE ● WE ARE THE CLAY, 2010 ●
36 x 25 inches (91.4 x 63.5 cm) ● 100% cotton,
thread; fused appliqué, machine quilted ●
Photo by artist

MARGARET DUNSMORE ● CLOSE TIES, 2007
● 45 x 34 inches (114.3 x 86.4 cm) ● Silk
and polyester ties, silk, cotton, buckle, colored
pencil; raw-edge machine appliquéd, turned-
hand appliquéd, machine pieced and quilted
● Photo by artist

GWEN MAYER ● BENEATH THE SURFACE OF A STEEL MILL, 2010 ● 48 x 36 inches (121.9 x 91.4 cm)
● Cotton, duck, organza, polyester, rayon, silk, suede cloth, assorted threads, printing ink, pens;
drawing, discharge printed, screen/brayer printed, dyed, appliquéd, hand embroidered, machine and
hand stitched ● Photo by Loris Bogue

INGE MARDAL and STEEN HOUGS ● THE CALM AFTER THE STORM, 2009 ● 64⁵/8 x 48¹³/16 inches (164.1 x 124 cm) ●
100% cotton; hand painted, machine quilted ● Photo by artists

ANN HORTON ● THREADS OF HER HANDS, 2010
● 44 x 37¹/₂ inches (111.8 x 95.3 cm) ● Cottons,
Guatemalan fabrics, cotton threads; machine pieced,
appliquéd, and quilted, digitized embroidery, hand-
guided machine embroidery ● Photo by artist

NORIKO NOZAWA ● CONCERTMISTRESS,
2009 ● 79¹/₈ x 79¹/₈ inches (201 x 201 cm)
● Cotton, lamé yarn, tulle lace, stencil paint;
machine appliquéd, pieced, and quilted ●
Photo by artist

MICHAEL A. CUMMINGS ● COTTON PICKING IN MECKLENBURG COUNTY, NORTH CAROLINA, 2008 ● 96 x 72 inches (243.8 x 182.9 cm) ● 100% cotton, cotton blends; appliquéd, machine sewn ● Photo by D. James Dee

CAROLYN CRUMP ● THE RIGHT TIME, 2010
● 50 x 46¹/₂ inches (118.1 x 127 cm) ● Cotton
fabric, cotton thread, felt; cotton batting, ink,
markers, pencil, dye, acrylic paint, buttons ●
Photo by Ash Wilson

HOLLIS CHATELAIN ● GOING TO THE MARKET, 1997
● 46 x 31 inches (116.8 x 78.7 cm) ● 100% cotton
fabric, cotton batting; hand dye painted, machine quilted
● Photo by Lynn Ruck

KATHY NIDA

KATHY NIDA'S ARCHETYPAL FIGURES LIVE in dreamlike landscapes where anything seems possible. The insides are on the outside; the outsides are home to cats, ravens, and snakes. The feet of her figures have often grown roots. Their bodies highlight the importance of the biological systems that support us, while the landscapes they populate include a wide range of symbolic icons representing environmental and political concerns. We may strive to create narratives to explain the inclusion of all these disparate elements, but the answers elude us. We can only visit in these scenes, not understand them.

ONE PAYCHECK, 2010 ● 38¹/₂ x 38 inches (97.8 x 96.5 cm) ● Commercial and hand-dyed cottons, ink; fused appliqué, machine stitched and quilted, hand inked ● Photo by artist

Art Background

I have an art degree. When I graduated, I started screen-printing on paper and exhibited my screen-prints until just after my son was born in 1996. I switched to nontoxic printing materials before I got pregnant, but it was really the time involved in making, printing, and cleaning the screens that pushed me into another medium. Quilting was something I could do in small stages while a kid was on the floor or in my lap. I could take parts of it with me to the park while the kids played. I could do it at soccer games and during practices. My mom was a weaver, and I think growing up with sewing and weaving all around me made me prefer the tactile nature of fabric.

Life-Science Teacher

My art has always had a connection to the Being of Woman, of having to be like Mother Earth without her resources, of trying to NOT be pregnant, then trying TO be pregnant, and then NOT again. That little group of organs, the uterus and the ovaries, rules a woman's life. So I've had the reproductive system in my drawings since college. The other parts started showing up later but became more prevalent

FULLY MEDICATED, 2011 ● 55 x 34¹/₂ inches (139.7 x 87.6 cm) ● Commercial and hand-dyed cottons, ink; fused appliqué, machine stitched and quilted, hand inked ● Photo by artist

UNTIED, 2008 ● 55 1/2 x 50 3/4 inches (141 x 128.9 cm) ● Commercial and hand-dyed cottons, colored pencil; fused appliqué, machine stitched and quilted ● Photo by artist

once I started teaching life science to kids. I know from life-drawing classes that what lies underneath determines how the stuff on top is shaped and will move, but I'm not sure what my drawings would look like now if I weren't teaching science.

I Can't Explain My Imagery

I can't really explain the imagery in my work. When I draw, one part of my brain deals with the drawing, with picking up stuff and deciding whether or not to put it in the drawing. It's not really connected to the part of my brain that goes to work and feeds the kids and cleans the bathroom. It's like it's over there, so I don't always have a clear idea of what the images mean, even to me.

I don't draw specific people; they're more like archetypes. Sometimes I have a vague idea of an image in my head, so I start with the eyes. The eyes tell me how the rest of the face is going to look. I do draw women much more often than men. Men's bodies aren't as fun to draw. I like the curves and hollows of a woman's body and the hint of fertility that's always there.

The cats and dogs are all mine. I've had six cats over my lifetime (three are alive right now), and they mean comfort and safety to me. I often look at their markings and try to draw them specifically. The birds all started out as ravens, the raven being a trickster, an ill omen, a sign of death or evil. I'm not sure all the birds are ravens anymore, though. They seem to talk the most, to provide a message.

The snakes are temptresses, another sign of evil, but they're also amazing biological organisms in terms

HERE, 2009 ● 54$^1/2$ x 46$^1/2$ inches (138.5 x 118.1 cm) ● Commercial and hand-dyed cottons, ink, cotton embroidery thread; fused appliqué, machine stitched and quilted, hand inked and embroidered ● Photo by artist

of their structures and how they eat and survive. My students will tell you they are also fun (and easy) to draw. They fit in small spaces well. They're another protector-spirit of sorts.

My Process

I draw a lot. I use a black, ultra-fine point Sharpie in a variety of sketchbooks. Sometimes I work on an idea for a show where I've seen a theme I like, but mostly I just draw, and a certain drawing will yell out to me that it wants to be a quilt. Then I enlarge it onto 11 x 17-inch (27.9 x 43.2 cm) sheets of paper, which I tape together. I number the pages of the enlarged drawing, turn each one over on a light box, and trace all the pieces onto Wonder Under fusible interfacing. When I draw the pieces, I keep in mind the fact that there will need to be extra fabric for overlapping them, so I have to think while I'm tracing about what's going to be on top and what's going to be underneath. I cut all the

pieces out with a little border around them and iron them onto my base fabrics.

I don't color my drawing except in my head. I have the background fabric and the large drawing out while I'm picking fabrics, and I audition all the colors in my head as I'm staring at the drawing. This process is easier if it's not interrupted too much, so I usually aim for long weekends or the longer breaks during the year. Otherwise, I have a hard time remembering how the partially colored drawing should look.

Once everything is ironed down, I trim all the pieces down to the lines. Then I iron them all together on nonstick appliqué sheets with the drawing underneath so I can see where the pieces fit together. I do this in parts: if there's a freestanding figure, I iron all its pieces together, then move on to the next freestanding part. Then I iron that whole mess down onto the background, stitch the pieces with clear thread

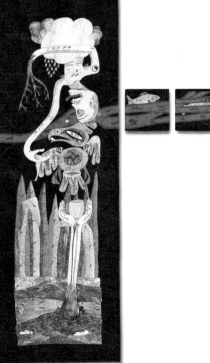

DISRUPTED, 2010 ● 70 1/2 x 118 inches (179.1 x 299.7 cm) ● Commercial and hand-dyed cottons, cotton embroidery thread; fused appliqué, machine stitched and appliquéd, hand embroidered ● Photo by Gregory Case

I WAS NOT WEARING A LIFE JACKET, 2010 ● 63¹/₂ x 73 inches (161.3 x 185.4 cm) ● Commercial and hand-dyed cotton and polyester fabrics, ink; fused appliqué, machine stitched and quilted, hand inked ● Photo by artist

using a small zigzag stitch, sandwich it, and quilt it. Usually, I start quilting with an outline in a darker color to emphasize the lines around the pieces, and then I'll quilt the background in other colors. I want the image to stand out, so I don't overquilt that part of it. I often add beads, hand embroidery, or hand inking after quilting to bring out certain elements of the quilt. I bind my quilts—I like that there's a final edge, like a frame.

Challenge of Fiber

For me, the biggest problem is that people associate fiber, especially quilt-based artwork, with craft, not art. The images I make are art, but people don't expect images like that in fabric. If I painted my images on canvas and put them in an art gallery, there would be a lot less fuss, but because I make them in fabric using quilt-making techniques and they can end up in quilt shows, the people who expect to see more traditional imagery are sometimes unhappy.

I don't like giving long explanations of particular images because I'm more interested in what the viewer sees when they look at my quilts. I do get annoyed with those who write them off because of the nudity. I want viewers to be intrigued. I like it when they come up to me and talk about what they see in my work, because I want it to be more about them than about me.

PAM RUBERT

A CARTOONISH CHARACTER WITH LONG, EXAGGERATED LIMBS and cat-eye glasses is the star in many of Pam RuBert's art quilts. The character, whose name is PaMdora, struggles with the trials and tribulations of modern life, from trying to do yoga without her morning coffee to fighting with modern technology. To create these witty scenes, RuBert uses a bright palette of bold colors, which she frames with black outlines created through careful appliqué and dense machine quilting. Look carefully to see the humor in her fabric choices and the symbols hidden in her quilting motifs. PaMdora's humorous take on life helps us to see the funnier aspects of our own.

YOGA 101: THE FRENCH PRESS POSE, 2011 ●
46 x 39 inches (116.8 x 99.1 cm) ● Cotton fabrics,
thread; layered, stitched ● Photo by artist

Who Is PaMdora?

In the first story quilt I made, I drew a woman with cat-eye glasses and a mid-century flip hairdo. She was part of a group of people watching the Voyager shuttle land on Mars, and she was reading a newspaper that had lots of jokes and funny stories about Martians.

My next quilt featured a character that looked like it had evolved from the Mars-watching lady. She was looking in dismay at a laptop computer, which was called PaMdora's Box, because out of it had come useful things as well as computer bugs and viruses in much the same way that the mythical Pandora's box released both good and evil.

That's when I knew the lady's name was PaMdora. She's looked pretty much the same in each quilt ever since, although, strangely, when I gain weight, her hips seem to get bigger, too. I like dressing her in different clothes, almost like you'd dress a doll, but she always wears cat-eye glasses that resemble the blue and brown ones I wore as a kid.

PARIS—WISH YOU WERE HAIR, 2008 ● 38 x 49 inches (96.5 x 124.5 cm) ● Cotton fabrics, thread; layered, stitched ● Photo by artist

TOKYO—WISH YOU WERE HAIR, 2010 ● 50 x 60 inches (127 x 152.4 cm) ● Cotton fabrics, thread; layered, stitched ● Photo by Russ RuBert

● Pam RuBert

TOWERS OF BABBLE, 2006 ● 57 x 85 inches (144.8 x 215.9 cm) ● Cotton fabrics, thread; layered, stitched ●
Photo by artist

People sometimes ask me about her face. She never smiles. I tried drawing a smile on her face once, and it looked sort of sickly, like she was trying to fake it. It's funny how much people like PaMdora. Often they'll tell me how much they relate to her. People often ask me if she's my alter ego, but I think of her more as my doppelgänger, a double who represents misfortune.

The Problem with Fiber

I can't relate to the term "fiber" because, to me, it sounds like something made out of rope. I can't relate to the term "textile" because it reminds me too much of tapestry and weaving. I don't like it when people label me as a quilter or even as a quilt artist, because I feel that I'm an artist who chooses to work sometimes with quilt materials and techniques and sometimes with other materials and techniques. However, I don't mind calling my work a quilt if it's truly a quilt. I guess that's an odd mix of attitudes.

Brain Magnet

Sometimes I run across words or puns that spark my interest. Once, while we were at an airport, my husband said, "Doesn't it seem like cell phones just encourage some people to babble incessantly about what they're doing?" I suddenly had a vision of cell phone towers being modern Towers of Babel.

A concept like that can get lodged in my brain and act like a little "brain magnet," just sitting there in the back of my mind, collecting and attracting any other pun, image, or character that's related or somehow fits. Eventually, this brain magnet becomes a big cluster of accumulated stuff.

I need this type of cluster of ideas and images to create, especially the big quilts, where there's a lot going on, because it gives me a lot of conceptual material to work with. And vice versa. As long as the brain magnet sits in my head, more and more stuff gets collected, and the quilt has to become bigger to handle all the concepts.

Importance of Color

I've noticed that if I don't regularly have injections of bright, bold color, I feel down, unenergetic, and uncreative. It's not just the intensity of color. I like to combine a lot of different colors, which probably explains some of my attraction to patchwork.

After I changed the curtains in my office so that they matched, I never wanted to go in there. I started getting really behind on paying my bills. So I replaced the curtains with some unhemmed pieces of fabric that were solid green, blue, and orange and slightly translucent, so that the light that comes through my south-facing window is multi-colored. Now walking into the room is almost like walking into a warm bath of color. I almost instantly feel more relaxed and happy.

I use a lot of color and also try to use unexpected combinations of patterns in my quilts, because I think it keeps the work lively. Sometimes I'll use a pattern for a humorous effect—to create a plaid pretzel or polka-dotted car. The interesting thing about patterns is that they can look like one color up close and a completely different color from far away. When I'm designing, I constantly walk towards and away from the design wall so I can see both effects. I also take a lot of photos in the process, because sometimes patterns can look completely different on camera than they do to the eye.

I pin all the parts of a quilt on my design wall until I've completely designed the whole piece, because each color of fabric affects the others. When I get

TANGO WITH A TECHNOPUS, 2010 ● 54 x 69 inches (137.2 x 175.3 cm) ● Cotton fabrics, thread; layered, stitched
● Photo by Russ RuBert

ST. LOUIS—WISH YOU WERE HAIR, 2008 ● 59 x 41 inches (149.9 x 104.1 cm) ● Cotton fabrics, thread; layered, stitched ● Photo by artist

YOGA 101: THE BANANA SPLIT POSE, 2006 ● 42 x 53 inches (106.7 x 134.6 cm) ● Cotton fabrics, thread; layered, stitched ● Photo by artist

the right combination, they seem to sing to me, so it's almost like I'm tuning a musical instrument, trying to get everything in harmony before I sew it together.

"Wish You Were Hair"

"Wish You Were Hair" is a pun I thought up long ago when I started collecting vintage travel postcards. I remembered how as a kid, we would go on car trips and buy postcards to send to my grandmother and my friends back home.

Doing loose sketches for this series is fun, and I try to do them in relaxed situations, while on vacation or floating on our pontoon boat. I like using color ink brush pens. I do the sketches fast, spending maybe less than five minutes on each sketch. Then I trace the drawing and blow it up into a working pattern.

St. Louis—Wish You Were Hair is a nostalgic piece for me because I was born in St. Louis. I drew a girl with a braided arch hairdo and started thinking about the McDonald's riverboat that used to be on the river

under the arch. But when I looked up the riverboat, I found out that it isn't there anymore. I felt sort of sad about the boat being gone. Even though I don't care about McDonald's, there's a sense of loss when unique icons disappear—it reminds us of our own mortality.

Poking Fun at Life

I pick topics and subjects that are a part of my life: supermarkets, yoga, stepping in puppy doo, crazy taxi drivers, cell phones, computer problems. Sometimes things that bother me build up into internal pressure or distress, and I have to blow off some steam. Turning those things into art, making fun of them, and taking control of my own little corner of the world inside my quilt are ways to deal with the pressure. I think people relate to that. Maybe they also have frustrations or things they think are crazy about our modern life. Maybe they can share a little in my sense of humor and enjoy the ride.

CAROL GODDU

WHAT TREMENDOUS ENERGY CAROL GODDU'S dancing figures have! They dance in the attic, they dance with vacuum cleaners, they dance in the park. Carefully researching the dance styles and costume details of different eras, Goddu scours a variety of sources to find the right materials and embellishments for creating historically accurate dance parties. Silhouetted figures and architectural elements are created from suede-like material, but the main dancers wear historically accurate clothing that's carefully constructed over lightweight interfacing or designed like flattened doll clothes with two layers seamed together. Settings add historical details or simply provide a dance floor—and everyone is dancing up a storm.

DANCE AS IF NO ONE IS WATCHING, 2009 ●
67 x 65 inches (170.2 x 165.1 cm) ● Cottons, synthetic suede; hand appliquéd, machine quilted and pieced ●
Photo by Alan McKenzie

Pictorial Quilts

When I started making pictorial quilts, I drew my imagery from the sixteenth- and seventeenth-century oil paintings of Holbein and van Dyck, with their lush details of rich wardrobes. I found that the accepted method of machine appliqué—flat shapes of fabric surrounded with satin stitch—was counterproductive for the fabrics I was working with. Van Dyck was truly a genius at portraying a three-dimensional satin gown in two-dimensional oils, but I was using an actual piece of satin. It seemed obvious that I should let the fabric drape freely, not lay it down flat and then stitch pretend folds into it.

Collections of Ideas

I'm always on the lookout for ideas and images that could become the subject of some future quilt. I collect both photos and line drawings. I reduce the photos to line drawings before making the actual patterns for my figures. Sometimes the collection process goes on for years before I get around to starting the quilt. Inevitably, I find that I have enough raw material for more than one quilt and must ruthlessly edit out a lot of really promising stuff.

MOULIN ROUGE, 1994 ● 72 x 58 inches (182.9 x 147.3 cm) ● Cottons, silks, lace, organza, trims; hand appliquéd and embroidered, machine appliquéd and quilted ● Photo by Alan McKenzie

TAPPING IN THE ATTIC, 1992 ● 68 x 80 inches (172.7 x 203.2 cm) ● Cottons, lamé, synthetic suede; hand appliquéd and embroidered, machine appliquéd and quilted ● Photo by Alan McKenzie

If my quilt contains only dancing figures without a room setting or social scene, I can include more of the dancing figures. I often frame these figures using a traditional quilt pattern called "Attic Windows"—hence the name of my tap dancer quilt, *Tapping in the Attic*. The frame provides the figures with a narrow stage on which to perform their dance. Otherwise, I might have fewer dancers with an array of onlookers and furniture. I enjoy the process equally either way.

All Kinds of Dance

I'm not a dancer myself. I briefly studied ballet as a child. In college, I took modern dance to satisfy a physical education requirement. It certainly beat out other options like field hockey.

When I made my first piece featuring dancers—a nineteenth-century couple waltzing—I had no plan to produce a series. But once I got started, I kept seeing more subjects that I wanted to use. I've portrayed Spanish fandango dancers, tango dancers, cancan dancers, Charleston dancers—even ancient Greek dancers celebrating the cult of Dionysus. I focus on capturing the sense of movement inherent in each form of dance.

Transparent Overlays

I prefer to find just the right fabric and use it as it is. I'm really committed to solving my problems with needle, thread, and fabric rather than paint. Instead of altering fabric with dyes, I prefer to use transparent overlays of organza or net. This means that I can experiment until I get the desired result because each trial is reversible and removable. This is vital, since I often work with small pieces of fabric that I have had on hand for years and may no longer be available.

I'm interested in historical accuracy—what someone might actually have worn to a nineteenth-century soiree or to the theatre in the 1920s. Buying specialty fabrics and trims has become more challenging over the years. Luckily, I've amassed a significant hoard that's become my primary supply source. Sometimes I get lucky—someone clears out their mother's house, finds a stash of vintage lace, and unloads it for 10 cents a yard.

Process for "Ode to Dionysus"

For *Ode to Dionysus*, I started with research, looking particularly at imagery from Greek vase paintings. Then I decided on the color scheme and pulled out all potential fabrics from my stash. The next step was to

ODE TO DIONYSUS, 2000 ● 62 x 76 inches (157.5 x 193 cm) ● Cottons, silks, metallic trims; hand appliquéd and embroidered, machine appliquéd and quilted ● Photo by Alan McKenzie

SERENADE, 2010 ● 49$^1/_2$ x 40 inches (125.8 x 101.6 cm) ● Cottons, synthetic suede, metallic trims; hand appliquéd and embroidered, machine appliquéd and quilted ● Photo by Alan McKenzie

determine the size range for the adult figures and to enlarge my selected figures to full size. I then hand embroidered the faces using DMC embroidery floss. (I recently discovered that there's a lower limit to how small I can successfully work. I drew the faces in the lower panel of *Serenade* with archival inks.) Working one panel at a time, I made costumes for the figures using hand appliqué. My technique is constantly evolving. My current method involves cutting exact shapes for each piece of clothing—a sleeve, a collar, a stocking—out of lightweight fusible interfacing. I fuse these shapes on the reverse side of the chosen fabric, cut out the shape plus seam allowance, and fold the seam allowance under the original

SOIREE, 1996 ● 64 x 76 inches (162.6 x 193 cm) ● Cottons, silks, lamé, synthetic suede, lace, feathers, metallic trims; hand appliquéd and embroidered, machine appliquéd and quilted ● Photo by Alan McKenzie

interfacing shape. I then have the desired shape with no raw edges and can appliqué this to the background.

When I'd completed all of the panels, I joined them together using lattice strips. I added the borders, including suede-like architectural details. Then I added a binding.

Evolution of Design

I'm not one of those quilters who has everything mapped out on ¼-inch graph paper before I start working in fabric. My design process is evolutionary. I start making figures relating to my theme and arrange and re-arrange them on my design wall.

A lot of revision goes on, both in the arrangement of the figures and within the details of the figures themselves. The faces that end up on a finished quilt may be the third or fourth versions. I save all the previous attempts and some of them end up on future quilts. The rest form a supply of teaching samples.

When a quilt is "finished," I let it hang in the studio so that I can tweak its details. I never feel that I end up achieving 100% of what I had in mind—it's always a compromise between what I can imagine and what I can actually create. Even when the work is sent off to meet some arbitrary deadline, I may still tweak it when it returns.

My Art Is My Escape

The positive energy that you see is pretty much only in the work. There's definitely an escapist element in this for me. When the challenges of daily life and the insanity displayed in the news threaten to overwhelm me, this wonderful fiber universe of my own making is ready and waiting. There, the sun is always shining and the people are ready to dance.

play

JULIE STERN BRANDON ● CHILDHOOD EXHILARATION, 2010 ●
$52^1/_2$ x $34^3/_4$ inches (133.5 x 88.3 cm) ● Microsuede, 100% cotton, wool,
inks, beads, shells; machine pieced and quilted ● Photo by Tim Fuss

KATHY YORK ● A FEW OF MY FAVORITE THINGS, 2009 ● 48 x 36 inches (121.9 x 91.4 cm) ● Batik, ink; whole cloth, machine quilted, hand lettering ● Photo by artist

CARYL BRYER FALLERT ● CHECKS AND BALANCES #1, 2010 ● 65 x 93 inches (165.1 x 236.2 cm) ● 100% cotton fabric, 100% cellulose batting; machine pieced and quilted ● Photo by artist

VALENTINA MAXIMOVA ● THE CLOWN, 2007 ●
32 x 20 inches (81.3 x 50.8 cm) ● 100% cotton,
linen; hand pieced, raw-edge appliqué, zigzag
stitched ● Photo by Pavel Karpov

SANDRA HANKINS ● O, 2010 ● 33 x 26 inches
(83.8 x 66 cm) ● 100% cotton fabric, organza, ink,
glitter; thread stitched, machine quilted ● Photo
by Sharon Mintry

MAGGIE DILLON ● THE BOYS, 2010 ● 45 x 60 inches (114.3 x 152.4) ● Batik fabric; thread work, machine appliquéd ●
Photo by artist

TANYA A. BROWN ● THE IMP, 2009 ● 24 x 35 inches (61 x 88.9 cm) ● 100% cotton, ink; machine quilted ● Photo by artist

KELLY LARAINE HENDRICKSON ● SKY GAZER, 2011 ● 9^{1}/$_{2}$ x 22^{3}/$_{4}$ inches (24.2 x 57.8 cm) ●
100% cotton batiks; raw-edge appliqué, machine quilted ● Photo by Tom Hendrickson

KATHLEEN KASTLES ● ELAINE, 2011 ●
24³/₄ x 13¹/₂ inches (62.9 x 34.3 cm) ●
100% cotton, acrylic inks with aloe vera gel
medium; whole cloth, machine quilted ●
Photo by José Morales

SUE KING ● ALL THE YOUNG DUDES, 2011 ●
36 x 15 inches (91.4 x 38.1 cm) ● 100% cotton,
commercial fabrics; hand dyed, machine quilted
and pieced ● Photo by Robert Colgan

TANYA A. BROWN ● FLOODED, 2011 ● 56¹/₂ x 45 inches (143.5 x 114.3 cm) ● Soy-sized cotton, watercolor, ink; machine quilted ● Photo by artist

ABOUT THE AUTHOR

Martha Sielman is the author of *Masters: Art Quilts, Volumes 1* and *2* (Lark Books, 2008 and 2011). She is the Executive Director of Studio Art Quilt Associates, Inc. (SAQA), the world's largest art quilt organization dedicated to advancing art quilting as a fine-art medium. Sielman's career in art quilts began in 1988, when she learned to quilt, and has included more than 20 years of work as a professional artist, author, lecturer, curator, juror, and arts administrator.

Since joining SAQA as Executive Director in 2004, Sielman has witnessed the explosive growth of art quilting, as well as growing interest in art quilts as a legitimate and collectible fine-art medium. The increasing popularity of art quilting is evidenced by SAQA's 2,900 members from more than 30 countries, by the explosion of art quilt exhibits around the globe, and by the blockbuster success of the *Masters: Art Quilts* books and exhibits. SAQA's receipt in 2010 of a Visual Arts grant from the National Endowment of the Arts also testifies to the growth and popularity of the medium.

Sielman has written articles about art quilts for *Quilting Arts Magazine, Quilter's Newsletter, Machine Quilting Unlimited,* and *Quilt Trends Magazine.* She curated the exhibits for *Masters: Art Quilts 1* and *Masters: Art Quilts 2,* which travelled extensively in the United States and abroad. She also curated the exhibit for *Art Quilt Portfolio: The Natural World.* Sielman has lectured at the International Quilt Festival and the Festival of Quilts and served as a juror for the 2009 NICHE Awards and for Pushing the Limits: New Expressions in Hooked Art.

Sielman lives in Storrs, Connecticut, with her husband, five children, and two cats.

ACKNOWLEDGMENTS

I would like to thank Ray Hemachandra at Lark Crafts for helping me to conceive and refine the concept for the *Art Quilt Portfolio* series. I'm also grateful to Amanda Carestio, my editor for this volume. Working with an editor who is also an art quilter has been exciting and rewarding. Both Amanda and production editor Julie Hale have been essential in making sure that the text in this book reads smoothly and without error. And nothing would have been accomplished without the organizational skills of editorial assistant Dawn Dillingham, who kept hundreds of images and contracts straight. Finally, I could not have written this book without the loving support of my husband, David, and my kids: Ben, Katie, Daniel, Lucy, and Jonathan. Thank you for doing the laundry, cooking dinner, and never complaining that I had to spend yet another afternoon at the computer.

Feature Artist Index

Gallery Artist Index